TANGRAM TALES

TANGRAM TALES

Story Theater Using the Ancient Chinese Puzzle

Dianne de Las Casas

Illustrated by Philip Chow

Teacher Ideas Press

An imprint of Libraries Unlimited

Westport, Connecticut • London

Library of Congress Cataloging-in-Publication Data

de Las Casas, Dianne.
    Tangram tales : story theater using the ancient Chinese puzzle / Dianne de Las Casas ; illustrated by Philip Chow.
        p. cm.
    Includes bibliographical references.
    ISBN 978–1–59158–652–4 (alk. paper)
    1. Storytelling. 2. Tangrams. 3. Teaching—Aids and devices. I. Title.
    LB1042.D395   2009
    372.67'7—dc22   2008037407

British Library Cataloguing in Publication Data is available.

Library of Congress Catalog Card Number: 2008037407
ISBN: 978–1–59158–652–4

First published in 2009

Libraries Unlimited/Teacher Ideas Press, 88 Post Road West, Westport, CT 06881
A Member of the Greenwood Publishing Group, Inc.
www.lu.com / www.teacherideaspress.com

Printed in the United States of America

The paper used in this book complies with the
Permanent Paper Standard issued by the National
Information Standards Organization (Z39.48–1984).

10 9 8 7 6 5 4 3 2 1

For Josie Chretien
My mother, my mentor, my hero
—Dianne de Las Casas

For Anita
Thank you for your support and understanding
—Philip Chow

Contents

Tangram Tales

Introduction

My work in storytelling has led me to become a teaching artist in the classroom. In my school residencies, I work for an extended period with the students, teaching them storytelling techniques. The residency often culminates in a student performance of the "Story Fest." Much of my residency work focuses on Story Theater. In my method of Story Theater, the entire class has the opportunity to participate.

Years ago, when my oldest daughter, Soleil (who as of this writing is 17 years old), was 10 years old, I bought her a Tangram book with a Tangram set. I had never worked with Tangrams and was amazed by how the paradoxical puzzle (it's profoundly simple and complex at the same time) captured her imagination. In addition to solving the Tangrams in the book, she began creating her own Tangrams (her favorite is the mermaid, which I always demonstrate to my students).

I began playing with the Tangrams and telling stories with the pictures, just for fun. Then it struck me: I could combine Tangrams with tales—Tangram Tales! I quickly began searching for resources. To my dismay, I found only one book that integrated Tangrams and stories—Valerie Marsh's Story Puzzles: Tales in the Tangram Tradition. The book, while wonderful (I am a big Valerie Marsh fan!), added other shapes to the traditional Tangram and hence wasn't quite what I was looking for. I wanted a story collection that uses the traditional seven-piece Tangram. I also found single stories such as Grandfather Tang's Story, by Ann Tompert, and Three Pigs, One Wolf, and Seven Magic Shapes, by Grace Maccarone. So I began rewriting traditional tales in my Story Theater format and integrating the Tangrams.

When I introduced this method to students and teachers, they went wild over the Tangram Tales process. Teachers loved the math and language arts aspect, and the students just loved creating with the Tangrams. It was a marriage made in heaven.

I am still amazed by the creativity I witness when students work with Tangrams. I love watching their imaginations ignite as they tell the stories and manipulate the shapes.

A very special thank-you to my daughter, Soleil, to whom I am deeply indebted. Soleil was my project leader, helping me research, draw, and create the many Tangrams in this book. I love you, Soleil! Thank you also to Nea Lewis, her good friend, who helped with the process.

A very big hug goes to Philip Chow, my artist (who happens to be from China). Phil is absolutely amazing and can always meet a deadline, even when he has a new baby in the house. As always, thank you so much, Phil.

Ignite your imagination and start toying with Tangrams. Happy Tangram Tales to you!

Warmly,

Dianne de Las Casas

www.storyconnection.net
dianne@storyconnection.net

Meeting Benchmarks with Tangram Tales

The following benchmarks are taken from the Standards for the English Language Arts by the National Council for the Teachers of English and the International Reading Association. Using Tangram Tales in the classroom allows students to meet the following language arts benchmarks:

- Students read a wide range of print and nonprint texts to build an understanding of texts, of themselves, and of the cultures of the United States and the world; to acquire new information; to respond to the needs and demands of society and the workplace; and for personal fulfillment. Among these texts are fiction and nonfiction, classic and contemporary works.
- Students apply a wide range of strategies to comprehend, interpret, evaluate, and appreciate texts. They draw on their prior experience, their interactions with other readers and writers, their knowledge of word meaning and of other texts, their word identification strategies, and their understanding of textual features (e.g., sound-letter correspondence, sentence structure, context, graphics).
- Students adjust their use of spoken, written, and visual language (e.g., conventions, style, vocabulary) to communicate effectively with a variety of audiences and for different purposes.
- Students apply knowledge of language structure, language conventions (e.g., spelling and punctuation), media techniques, figurative language, and genre to create, critique, and discuss print and nonprint texts.
- Students develop an understanding of and respect for diversity in language use, patterns, and dialects across cultures, ethnic groups, geographic regions, and social roles.
- Students participate as knowledgeable, reflective, creative, and critical members of a variety of literacy communities.
- Students use spoken, written, and visual language to accomplish their own purposes (e.g., for learning, enjoyment, persuasion, and the exchange of information).

The following benchmarks are taken from the Standards for School Mathematics (Geometry) by the National Council for Teachers of Math. Using *Tangram Tales* in the classroom allows students to meet the following math benchmarks:

- Analyze characteristics and properties of two- and three-dimensional geometric shapes and develop mathematical arguments about geometric relationships;
- Specify locations and describe spatial relationships using coordinate geometry and other representational systems;
- Apply transformations and use symmetry to analyze mathematical situations; use visualization, spatial reasoning, and geometric modeling to solve problems.

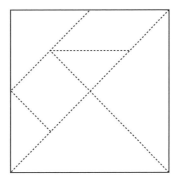

History of Tangrams

Though the exact history of the Tangram is unknown, it is believed to have originated in China. The Tangram consists of seven geometric pieces: two small isosceles right triangles, a medium-sized isosceles right triangle, two large isosceles right triangles, a square, and a parallelogram. When the pieces are in "resting shape," they form a perfect square. To begin puzzling, all seven geometric shapes must be used without overlapping to create shapes such as people, animals, and other objects. According to Webster's Unabridged Dictionary from 1986, a Tangram is "a Chinese toy made by cutting a square of thin wood, or other suitable material, into seven pieces, these pieces being capable of combination in various ways, so as to form a great number of different figures."

Legend says that there was once a Chinese man named Tan. His greatest possession in the world was a beautiful square ceramic tile he created. On his way to show the Emperor his creation, Tan tripped. The tile fell and broke into seven pieces. Tan spent the rest of his life trying to form his perfect square but never succeeded. His efforts, however, created many beautiful shapes that have inspired people since.

The Tangram Tales Story Theater Process

Introduction to Story Theater

Story Theater is the narration of events through dramatic performance. In Story Theater, the storyteller performs or dramatizes a story through vocal inflections, facial expressions, and body movement. In my method of Story Theater, everyone has a part. Individual students are chosen for roles as storytellers, and the rest of the students participate in the story chorus. In addition, with the Tangram Tales Story Theater method, individual students are chosen as Tangram artists. The dynamic combination of storytelling and Tangram art makes Tangram Tales Story Theater fun to participate in and fun to watch. There is no one right way to tell a story. Every method has value. With that in mind, storytelling and Tangram Tales Story Theater are perfect for students with varied learning styles to communicate their creativity.

Before I explain how Tangram Tales Story Theater works and how to implement it in the classroom, I would like to share some important techniques that will help your students acclimate to the atmosphere of Tangram Tales Story Theater.

Establishing an Environment of Trust

To break the ice with students, I begin telling a Tangram Tale. The act of storytelling is an intimate art and allows the students to get to know me better, thus allowing them to trust me. You may use the tales provided in this book or research some Tangrams and create your own stories.

Trust is very important in Story Theater. Storytellers often use drama to expose themselves and their emotions in a new way. It is the same for students. Some students may have never role-played or acted out a part and may feel uncomfortable doing so in front of their peers. In addition, students who are not accustomed to sharing their artwork in a community setting may feel self-conscious.

To establish an environment of trust, I introduce the "Classroom Contract," an agreement for grades three and up that enforces respect and prevents teasing. It is read orally, and at the end of each statement, the students say, "I agree." It helps set expectations and guidelines for the duration of my work with the students.

Classroom Contract

The number one rule is RESPECT.

- Respect fellow classmates—I will respect my classmates at all times. I will not laugh at them, make fun of them, or make them feel bad.
- Respect teacher—I will respect [Teacher's Name] by listening to her and following directions. Failure to do so will result in a behavior report [or other means of discipline suited to your school's environment].
- Respect other people's property—I will respect the property of my fellow classmates and my teacher(s). I will take care of borrowed items and put them back where they belong.

I find that an oral contract suffices, but you can add a signature line and have each student sign the contract. If the class becomes unruly, I simply pull out the Classroom Contract and issue a gentle reminder.

Introducing Tangram Tales Story Theater to Your Students

Tangram Tales Story Theater involves not only the dramatization of stories but also a visual art element. It is a great way to incorporate language arts, mathematics, social studies, and visual arts simultaneously. Students strengthen their knowledge of geometry, sequencing skills, and presentation skills, and they learn about other cultures.

Group Tangram Tales

Tangram Tales may be used in many ways in the classroom. Performing Tangram Tales as a group allows the whole class to present a story and is a good way to introduce Tangram Tales when you are short on time. Each student will need construction paper or foam sheets, scissors, a Tangram pattern and Tangram Tales, or a Tangram puzzle. Have students follow the Tangram pattern and cut out their puzzle pieces. If you are working with younger students, it is best to have the Tangram pieces already cut out. I like to use the pieces made of foam, but educational catalogs have many types of classroom sets available. For demonstration purposes on magnetic boards, I use large magnetic Tangram pieces. My set, which I purchased from an online educational store, comes with six different colored sets of Tangrams in eight-inch squares.

Select a story and read it out loud to the class so that students can familiarize themselves with it. Ask them to visualize the scenes of the story. Some students will tell the story while others, who have been chosen as Tangram artists, will illustrate their scene of the story with Tangrams.

Photocopy your selected story or write your own story and print it. Choose students to play the parts of the storytellers, the chorus, and the Tangram artists. Once the parts have been assigned, the class can begin rehearsing. Although students can read their lines, I encourage them to tell their part of the story, which does not mean memorizing their lines. Their part does not have to match the lines of the story exactly as long as they are conveying what is in their scene.

It typically takes four class periods for the process. In the first class period, the teacher tells the story, assigns the story and Tangram parts, and works on the Tangram illustrations. In the second period, students learn the story and create the Tangram illustrations. Students spend the third period rehearsing their Tangram Tale and then present it in the fourth.

Storyteller and Tangram Artist working together.

Before beginning the Tangram Tales Story Theater process, allow the students to familiarize themselves with Tangrams. Pass out Tangram sets to each student and have them manipulate the shapes, creating the puzzles found in the "Reproducible Tangram Figures" section of this book. For older students, you may also teach them how to cut out their own Tangram set by using the "Create a Tangram without a Pattern" instructions. Students should manipulate the pieces, familiarizing themselves with the names of the shapes: triangle, square, parallelogram.

When the artists are putting together their Tangram pictures, allow them to be imaginative and combine colors. For instance, in the tale "Windbird and the Sun," the students used different-colored Tangrams to create the rainbow in the story. When working with double Tangrams (two Tangrams in the same scene), have each Tangram artist use two colors.

Tangram Tip: If you are working with a precut magnetic set, like the one I use, you may need to create another parallelogram in the opposite direction to account for puzzles that have the parallelogram facing the opposite way. You may do this by purchasing foam, tracing the parallelogram, cutting it out, and affixing a magnet to the opposite side.

Student-Created Tangram Tales

In the student-created Tangram Tales method, students tell their own stories. They may learn one of the stories in this book and use a magnetic board to tell their stories to the class.

Alternatively, students may rewrite folktales, create their own versions, research Tangrams to coincide with their stories, and create their own Tangram Tales.

Connecting with the Curriculum

Tangrams and Geometry

With prekindergarten through second grades, I share a Tangram Tale and allow the students to guess what picture each Tangram puzzle forms in the story. Then I familiarize the students with the various shapes of the Tangram—the triangle, the square, and the parallelogram. I pass out foam Tangrams to each student and instruct the following:

1. How many triangles are there in a Tangram?
2. Find the square.
3. Find the large triangle.
4. Find the smallest triangle.
5. Find the parallelogram.
6. Make a square using two pieces.
7. Tangram rules—When putting together a Tangram puzzle, all seven pieces must be used, no pieces may overlap, and each piece must touch at least one other piece (generally).

Using reproducible Tangram figures, students work on manipulating the Tangrams, becoming more familiar with their shapes by piecing together various Tangram puzzles.

I also ask the students to create their own Tangrams. When they have finished, you can have them trace around the Tangram pieces so that they have a record of their Tangram puzzle creation. A first-grader named Carlton created the following Rocket Tangram.

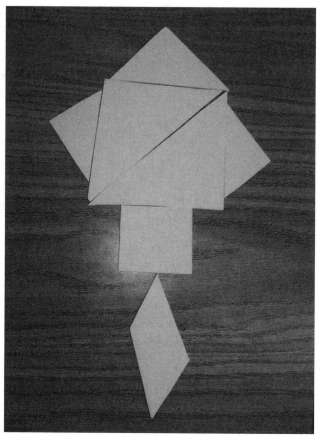

Rocket Tangram created by first grader.

For grades 3–6, I begin by placing the Tangram on the board in the shape of a square. I explain that a Tangram is an ancient Chinese puzzle consisting of various geometric shapes: the triangle, the square, and the parallelogram. I then tell the story "The Legend of the Tangram." Next, I show how the Tangram can be manipulated into various pictures, which usually elicits a "Wow!" or "Cool!" from the students.

To introduce geometric concepts, I ask the students, How many shapes are on this board? It is a trick question, and most of the students usually answer seven because they see seven figures on the board. The correct answer, however, is three: the triangle, the square, and the parallelogram.

Using the large triangle, I explain how the geometric angles of each shape contribute to make the Tangram a perfect square. The isosceles right triangles have two 45° angles and one 90° angle, adding up to 180°. The 45° angle is an acute angle, and the 90° angle is a right angle. I demonstrate the symmetry of the Tangram triangles by dissecting one-half and showing how the two halves still remain isosceles right triangles.

I explain that the square and the parallelogram are quadrilaterals, meaning that they are polygons with four sides. The square is a quadrilateral with four right angles and four equilateral sides. The parallelogram is a quadrilateral that has two opposite sides that are parallel.

Through the use of the Tangram, the students seem to better grasp and appreciate the geometric concepts that are introduced. The Tangram allows them to see how geometry works in real life through a tangible manipulative.

Tangram Vocabulary

Acute angle—An angle measuring less than 90°.

Angle—An angle consists of two rays that share a common endpoint. The common endpoint of the two rays (where the rays meet) is called the vertex of the angle. The two rays are called the sides of the angle.

Congruent triangles—Triangles that have the same size and shape. Corresponding angles have the same measure, and corresponding sides have the same length.

Degree—The measurement of the size of an angle.

Equilateral—Equal in length.

Isosceles triangle—A triangle with two equal sides.

Obtuse angle—An angle measuring more than 90° but less than 180°.

Parallelogram—A quadrilateral (a four-sided shape) that has two pairs of opposite sides that are parallel.

Polygon—means "many sided."

Quadrilateral—A four-sided polygon (such as a square, a rectangle, a parallelogram, a rhombus, or a trapezoid).

Right angle—An angle measuring exactly 90°.

Right triangle—A triangle with one right (90°) angle.

Symmetry—A design has symmetry if you can move the entire design by either rotation or reflection and the design appears unchanged.

Trapezoid—A four-sided quadrilateral with one pair of parallel sides.

Tangrams as Writing Prompts

Tangram figures are a great segue into a writing exercise. Form a Tangram figure on the board and have the students write a paragraph about the Tangram puzzle. For instance, if you create a rooster, the students would write a short story about a rooster.

Another way to use the Tangram in a writing exercise is to give each student a Tangram set. Have the student configure his or her own Tangram puzzle and write a short story about it. Include a picture of the Tangram with the story.

Culminating Event—The Tangram Tales Story Fest (Performance-Based Assessment)

In the culminating event, students perform their Tangram Tales Story Theater. While Tangram Tales are great for in-class use, creating a gradewide or schoolwide Story Fest allows the student storytellers to share their efforts with an appreciative audience. Gradewide Tangram Story Fests, where each class performs for its peers, develop an atmosphere of respect and support because each student performs during the Story Fest. Another option is to have the class perform for lower grades. The younger students admire the older students, and the older students will come away with a sense of accomplishment. Still another alternative is a Family Night Tangram Story Fest, where students proudly perform for their parents, grandparents, and other family members.

Tangram Tales is an exciting form of performance that works well in classroom settings as well as for larger audiences. Students have the opportunity to shine. Following their performance, reward the students by hosting a reception in their honor or passing out award stickers or certificates. Of course, the most rewarding part of Tangram Tales is the process itself. Seeing students performing their stories and creating Tangrams together is a fulfilling experience. You can

Student creating "Bee" Tangram.

be proud that you and your class have kept the age-old tradition of Tangram Tales alive and well.

Suggested Criteria for the Culminating Event

Have the students self-assess and answer the following questions:

Student creating "House" Tangram.

- Did students fulfill the task?
- Did students enunciate story lines clearly?
- Did students use different elements of characterization?
- Did students cooperate and interact with members of the group?
- Did students perform with focus and clarity?
- Did students express the different energies with strong intention and flow?
- Do the Tangrams enhance the delivery of the story?

Student creating "Candle" Tangram.

- Did each member of the group deliver his or her part enthusiastically?
- Does the group present a cohesive story?

When coaching students through the process, give direction through suggestion rather than telling the students how to perform their roles.

Assessment

Groups assess themselves in terms of the above criteria. Discuss with them what they feel they did well, what they might change, and what they could add or develop.

Lesson Extensions and Other Connections

- Have students write a paragraph about their feelings for the activity.
- Ask students what part of the lesson they enjoyed the most.
- Ask students if they enjoyed working individually, with partners, or as a group.
- Note how students come together to create an ensemble piece.

Research a folktale and have the class adapt it for its own Tangram Tales Story Theater. Assign the parts of researcher, script writers, editors, and Tangram researchers. Critique and evaluate the finished script as a group.

Reproducible Tangram Patterns

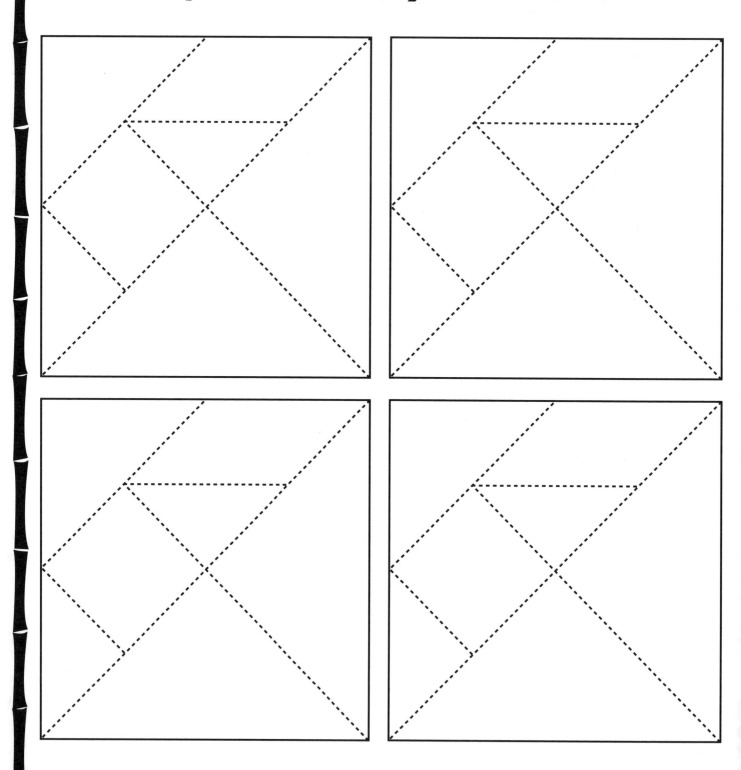

Reproducible Tangram Figures

Boat	Camel	Candle 1	Candle 2
Cat	Dancer 1	Dancer 2	Duck
Fairy	Farm House	Fish	Girl Running
Horse and Rider	Bucking Horse	House	Rabbit 1
Rabbit 2	Spinning Top	Swan	Vase

How to Cut a Tangram without a Pattern

Tangram

2   Large triangles   2   Small triangles   1   Square

1   Medium triangle   1   Parallelogram

Instructions

1. Start with a rectanglar sheet of paper. Make it into a square.

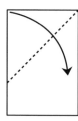

Cut off excess.

2. Cut into 2 triangles.

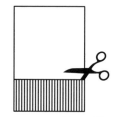

3. Cut piece A in half. Piece A will have 2 triangles. Those are done. Set them aside.

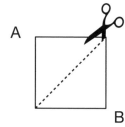

2 large triangles.

4. Now work with piece B. Make a crease by folding the top point to the bottom edge. Cut on the crease.

You will have 1 medium triangle.

5. You should have a trapezoid. From this piece, you will create 1 small triangle. Fold and cut on the crease.

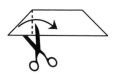

1 small triangle

6. Now you will create a square. Fold and cut on the crease.

1 square

7. From the remaining piece, you will create the second small triangle. Fold and cut on the crease.

1 small triangle

8. You are left with a parallelogram. Now you are DONE!

9. The tangram pieces:

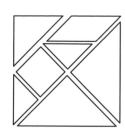

From *Tangram Tales: Story Theater Using the Ancient Chinese Puzzle* by Dianne de Las Casas. Westport, CT: Teacher Ideas Press. Copyright © 2009.

TANGRAM TALES

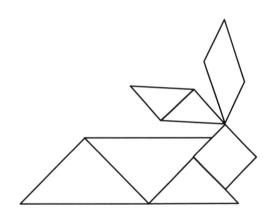

The Bossy Rooster
Cuba

Storyteller 1: There was once a very bossy rooster. He was on his way to the wedding of his Uncle Perico, Uncle Parrot.

Tangram: (Rooster)

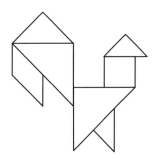

Chorus: I'm going to the wedding of Uncle Perico.
I'm going to the wedding of Uncle Perico.

Storyteller 2: Rooster was handsome and elegant. On the way, he saw a kernel of corn. He wanted to eat without dirtying his beak. He bent down and ate it up! El gallito said, "¡Ay, que rico! But I've dirtied mi pico (my beak)! And I cannot go to the wedding of Uncle Perico!"

Tangram: (Parrot)

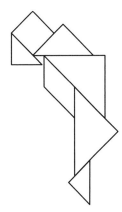

Storyteller 3: Just then, he saw the grass on the side of the road. He said, "Grass, clean mi pico so that I can go to the wedding of Uncle Perico." But Grass said,

Chorus: I don't want to. You're too bossy!

Tangram: (Grass)

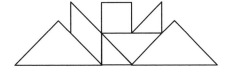

From *Tangram Tales: Story Theater Using the Ancient Chinese Puzzle* by Dianne de Las Casas. Westport, CT: Teacher Ideas Press. Copyright © 2009.

Storyteller 4:   Rooster saw a goat and he ordered, "Goat, eat the grass so that she will clean mi pico so that I can go to the wedding of Uncle Perico." But Goat said,

Chorus: I don't want to. You're too bossy!

Tangram: (Goat)

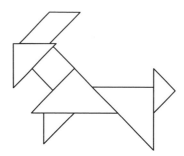

Storyteller 5:   Rooster then found a stick and he ordered, "Stick, hit the goat so that he will eat the grass so that she will clean mi pico so that I can go to the wedding of Uncle Perico." But Stick said,

Chorus: I don't want to. You're too bossy!

Tangram: (Stick)

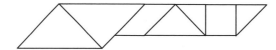

Storyteller 6:   A little while later, Rooster found the fire and he ordered, "Fire, burn the stick so that he will hit the goat so that he will eat the grass so that she will clean mi pico so that I can go to the wedding of Uncle Perico." But Fire said,

Chorus: I don't want to. You're too bossy!

Tangram: (Fire)

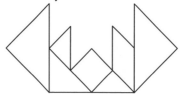

Storyteller 7: Now, Rooster was in a big hurry. He found the water and he ordered, "Water, quench the fire so that he will burn the stick so that he will hit the goat so that he will eat the grass so that she will clean mi pico so that I can go to the wedding of Uncle Perico." But Water said,

Chorus: I don't want to. You're too bossy!

Tangram: (Water)

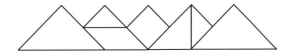

Storyteller 8: Poor little rooster! He didn't know what to do. He said, "Perhaps they are right. Maybe I *am* too bossy."
He looked up and he saw the sun smiling down upon him. Rooster smiled back. He remembered the magic word, please, and asked very sweetly, "Sun, can you please help me?"

Tangram: (Sun)

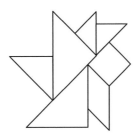

Storyteller 9: "Please dry the water so that he will quench the fire so that he will burn the stick so that he will hit the goat so that he will eat the grass so that she will clean mi pico so that I can go to the wedding of Uncle Perico."
Sun answered, "With pleasure."

Storyteller 10: When the sun began drying the water, the water began quenching the fire, the fire began burning the stick, the stick began hitting the goat, the goat began eating the grass, and the grass cleaned Rooster's beak.

Tangram: (Rooster)

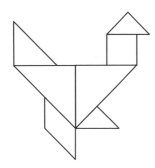

From *Tangram Tales: Story Theater Using the Ancient Chinese Puzzle* by Dianne de Las Casas. Westport, CT: Teacher Ideas Press. Copyright © 2009.

Storyteller 11: So, remembering his manners, Rooster thanked his friend, Sun, with a very joyous "¡Quiquiriqui!" and off he rushed to the wedding of Uncle Perico. To this day, Rooster greets Sun every morning with a joyous "¡Quiquiriqui!"

Chorus: I'm going to the wedding of Uncle Perico.
I'm going to the wedding of Uncle Perico.

The Cat and the Rooster
Ukraine

Storyteller 1: Once upon a time, Cat and Rooster were the best of friends. They lived together in a little hut in the midst of the forest. Cat would play his fiddle while Rooster would sing,

Chorus: What great friends we'll always be.
I have you and you have me!

Tangram: (Cat)

Storyteller 2: Every day, Cat would forage for food in the forest while Rooster ruled the roost. Cat said, "It's dangerous in the forest. Fox is always on the prowl. Stay inside."

Tangram: (Rooster)

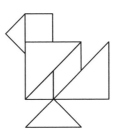

Storyteller 3: One day, Cat went to the forest as usual, foraging for food. Rooster promised to stay inside, but as he looked out the window, he noticed what a beautiful day it was. Spring was in the air, and flowers bloomed everywhere. He thought, "It won't hurt to step outside for a moment."

Tangram: (Flower)

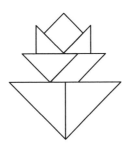

Storyteller 4: Sure enough, as soon as Rooster set foot outside, crafty Fox pounced. He caught Rooster and carried him away. Rooster cried,

Chorus: Cock-a-doodle-doo, Cock-a-doodle-doo!
My friend Cat, I really need you!

Tangram: (Fox)

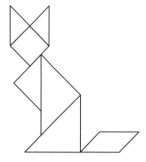

Storyteller 5: When Cat returned later that evening, he saw that Rooster was gone. He guessed what happened. "I hope I'm not too late," Cat thought as he raced to Fox's house. Inside, he heard Rooster crying,

Tangram: (House)

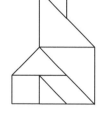

Chorus: Cock-a-doodle-doo, Cock-a-doodle-doo!
My friend Cat, I really need you!

Storyteller 6: Fox was out hunting and left his five children at home. Fox warned them not to let anyone into the house. Fox was cunning, but Cat was even cleverer. He said, "Children, your father warned you not to let anyone in, but he didn't say you couldn't come out." He began to play a tune on his fiddle.

Chorus: What great friends we'll always be.
I have you and you have me!

Tangram: (Foxes dancing)

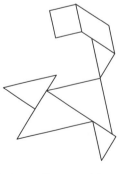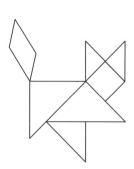

Storyteller 7: The fox children could not resist the catchy song. One by one, they came out and danced. And one by one, Cat caught each of them in a sack. Then Cat went inside the house and rescued his friend, Rooster.

Tangram: (Cat and Rooster)

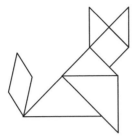 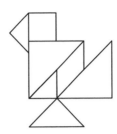

Storyteller 8: Cat and Rooster were the best of friends. They lived together in a little hut in the midst of the forest. Cat would play his fiddle while Rooster would sing,

Chorus: What great friends we'll always be.
I have you and you have me!

The Goat in the Jalapeño Patch
Mexico

Storyteller 1: Pedro had a pet goat. The goat was always hungry and ate everything.

Tangram: (Goat)

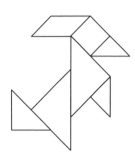

Chorus: Chomp, chomp, chomp. Chomp, chomp, chomp.
That goat eats too much!

Storyteller 2: To stop the goat from eating everything, Pedro and his mama took the goat to Grandfather's jalapeño patch. Grandfather said, "My jalapeños are so hot that just one lick will set his mouth on fire and will cure him for good."

Tangram: (Pepper)

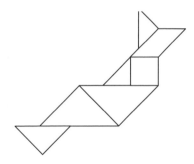

Storyteller 3: They set the goat in the middle of the patch. The goat began sniffing. When he found the biggest, juiciest jalapeño, he stopped. He bent down and took a big bite. Pedro and his family waited for the goat to run out of the patch, but he kept chewing and chewing and chewing.

Tangram: (Goat)

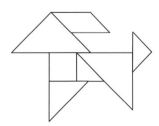

From *Tangram Tales: Story Theater Using the Ancient Chinese Puzzle* by Dianne de Las Casas. Westport, CT: Teacher Ideas Press. Copyright © 2009.

Chorus: Chomp, chomp, chomp. Chomp, chomp, chomp.
That goat eats too much!

Storyteller 4: When he was finished with that jalapeño, he found another one. He took a big bite and kept chewing and chewing and chewing.

Tangram: (Pepper)

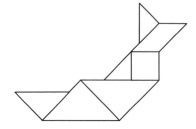

Chorus: Chomp, chomp, chomp. Chomp, chomp, chomp.
That goat eats too much!

Storyteller 5: Over and over again, the goat found a jalapeño, took a big bite, and kept chewing and chewing and chewing, until he had eaten a quarter of the jalapeño patch!

Tangram: (Goat)

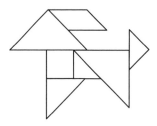

Chorus: Chomp, chomp, chomp. Chomp, chomp, chomp.
That goat eats too much!

Storyteller 6: Then Grandfather marched into the patch and tried to push the goat out. But the goat just raised his hind legs, kicked, and sent Grandfather flying out of the jalapeño patch. Dog was walking by when he heard the commotion. He asked, "What's wrong?" Grandfather answered, "That goat keeps chewing and chewing and chewing! He'll eat my whole jalapeño patch if we don't stop him!"

Tangram: (Dog)

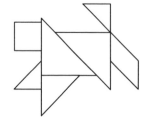

The Goat in the Jalapeño Patch

Chorus: Chomp, chomp, chomp. Chomp, chomp, chomp.
That goat eats too much!

Storyteller 7:   So Dog went into the jalapeño patch and barked furiously. But that didn't scare the goat. He raised his hind legs and kicked Dog right out of the patch. Then Goat kept chewing and chewing and chewing. Horse was walking by when he heard the commotion. He asked, "What's wrong?" Grandfather answered, "That goat keeps chewing and chewing and chewing! He'll eat my whole jalapeño patch if we don't stop him!"

Tangram: (Horse)

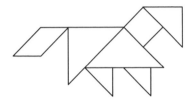

Chorus: Chomp, chomp, chomp. Chomp, chomp, chomp.
That goat eats too much!

Storyteller 8:   So Horse went into the jalapeño patch, stomped on the ground, and neighed furiously. But that didn't scare the goat. He raised his hind legs and kicked Horse right out of the patch. Then Goat kept chewing and chewing and chewing. Bull was walking by when he heard the commotion. He asked, "What's wrong?" Grandfather answered, "That goat keeps chewing and chewing and chewing! He'll eat my whole jalapeño patch if we don't stop him!"

Tangram: (Bull)

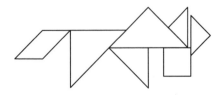

Chorus: Chomp, chomp, chomp. Chomp, chomp, chomp.
That goat eats too much!

The Goat in the Jalapeño Patch (Page 4)

Storyteller 8: So Bull went into the jalapeño patch and charged at the goat. But that didn't scare the goat. He raised his hind legs and kicked Bull right out of the patch. Then Goat kept chewing and chewing and chewing. Bee was buzzing by when she heard the commotion. She asked, "What's wrong?" Grandfather answered, "That goat keeps chewing and chewing and chewing! He'll eat my whole jalapeño patch if we don't stop him!"

Tangram: (Bee)

Chorus: Chomp, chomp, chomp. Chomp, chomp, chomp.
That goat eats too much!

Storyteller 8: Bee said, "I can get him out." Grandfather said, "You're too small!" But Bee insisted. So she went into the jalapeño patch and climbed onto the goat's hind legs, stopping on his backside. The goat didn't even notice her, because she was so small. Then she stung him. The goat let out a loud yelp and ran out of the jalapeño patch.

Tangram: (Goat running)

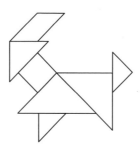

Chorus: Buzz, buzz, buzz. Buzz, buzz, buzz.
That bee's sting was too much!

Storyteller 9: Pedro, Mama, and Grandfather were happy. Grandfather said, "That little bee carries a big sting!" Bee smiled as Grandfather gave her a big, juicy jalapeño pepper. From that time forward, the goat ate only what he was fed, and everyone remarked that Pedro had such a nice pet.

From *Tangram Tales: Story Theater Using the Ancient Chinese Puzzle* by Dianne de Las Casas. Westport, CT: Teacher Ideas Press. Copyright © 2009.

Grandfather Rabbit and the Foolish Fox
Native American

Storyteller 1: Long ago there lived a herd of rabbits. One day, two rabbits were playing near the lake.

Tangram: (Two rabbits looking at each other)

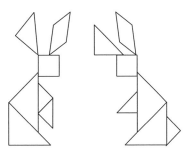

Storyteller 2: A short while later, a hungry fox sauntered by.
Tangram: (Fox walking)

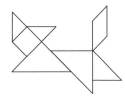

Storyteller 3: When he saw the rabbits, his stomach growled. "I will catch one for my supper!" he cried. He began chasing a rabbit around.

Chorus: Run, rabbit, run. Run! Run, rabbit, run. Run!
Run, rabbit, run. Run! Rabbit run fast!

Tangram: (Rabbit running)

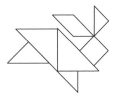

Storyteller 4: Fox had to stop to catch his breath. He could not catch the rabbit! The rabbit was too fast.

Tangram: (Fox resting)

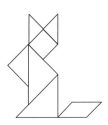

From *Tangram Tales: Story Theater Using the Ancient Chinese Puzzle* by Dianne de Las Casas. Westport, CT: Teacher Ideas Press. Copyright © 2009.

Grandfather Rabbit and the Foolish Fox (Page 2)

Storyteller 5:   Meanwhile, the rabbits had a meeting. Grandfather Rabbit said, "We need to trick that fox or he will continue to bother us." The other rabbits agreed and they formed a plan.

Tangram: (Two rabbits looking at each other)

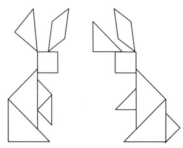

Storyteller 6:   The next day, Grandfather Rabbit approached Fox. He said, "Fox, I would like to challenge you to a race. If you beat me, you can eat me. If I beat you, you will leave the rabbits alone." Fox agreed.

Tangram: (Rabbit and Fox talking)

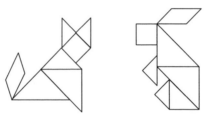

Storyteller 7:   The following day, Grandfather Rabbit and Fox raced. Fox ran as fast as he could.

Tangram: (Fox running)

Storyteller 8:   No matter how fast Fox ran, Grandfather Rabbit was always ahead of him.

Chorus: Run, rabbit, run. Run! Run, rabbit, run. Run!
Run, rabbit, run. Run! Rabbit run fast!

Tangram: (Rabbit running)

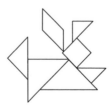

From *Tangram Tales: Story Theater Using the Ancient Chinese Puzzle* by Dianne de Las Casas. Westport, CT: Teacher Ideas Press. Copyright © 2009.

Grandfather Rabbit and the Foolish Fox

Storyteller 9: Fox ran a little faster.

Tangram: (Fox running)

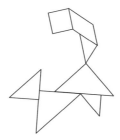

Storyteller 9: But no matter how fast Fox ran, Grandfather Rabbit was always ahead.

Tangram: (Rabbit running)

Chorus: Run, rabbit, run. Run! Run, rabbit, run. Run!
Run, rabbit, run. Run! Rabbit run fast!

Storyteller 10: Finally, Fox gave up. He said, "Grandfather Rabbit might be old, but he sure is fast." He lost the race. He promised to leave the rabbits alone.

Storyteller 11: Now the rabbits play freely near the lake. They always talk about the day they tricked Fox by hiding along the race route. To Fox, one rabbit looked like another, so he didn't know that he was racing more than one rabbit! And that is how Fox was outfoxed by a bunch of bunnies!

Chorus: Run, rabbit, run. Run! Run, rabbit, run. Run!
Run, rabbit, run. Run! Rabbit run fast!

Tangram: (Rabbits running)

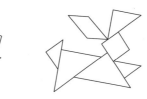

From *Tangram Tales: Story Theater Using the Ancient Chinese Puzzle* by Dianne de Las Casas. Westport, CT: Teacher Ideas Press. Copyright © 2009.

Grandmother Spider
Native American

Storyteller 1:   Long ago, the animals of the northern lands lived in darkness. Everything was fine for a while, until the animals began bumping into each other. Owl called a meeting of all the animals.

Tangram: (Owl)

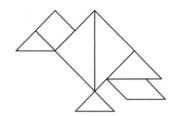

Storyteller 2:   Owl said, "We must do something about this darkness." Crow was the first to speak. He said, "Caw! Caw! I have heard of a place far away called 'The Land of the Sun People.' There, they have this thing called light. Light is so bright that everyone can see each other."

Tangram: (Crow)

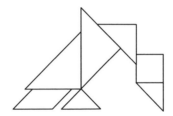

Storyteller 3:   Owl said, "Perhaps we can go to these people and ask them to share their light with us." Just then, crafty, cunning Fox crept forward. He said, "No! We can't just ask for the light. They won't just give us the light. We must snatch a piece of the light and bring it back!" Owl did not believe this was right, but Fox was so convincing that he persuaded all the animals to go along with his plan. Then Owl called,

Chorus: Who, who, who will go?

Tangram: (Fox)

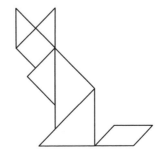

Storyteller 4: Possum stepped forward and said, "I will go. I will go to The Land of the Sun People and bring back the light. I can hide the light beneath my bushy tail." So the animals agreed, and Possum set off for The Land of the Sun People.

Chorus: He journeyed long, he traveled far.
Until he came to a place as bright as a star.
A place that was protected by guards.

Tangram: (Possum)

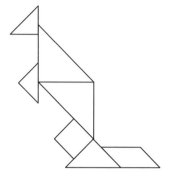

Storyteller 5: When the guards were not looking, Possum ran and snatched a piece of the light. He hid it under his bushy tail and began traveling home. He was nearly home when he felt

Chorus: A tickle, a tingle, a sizzle, a singe!
Possum's big bushy tail was on fire!

Tangram: (Fire)

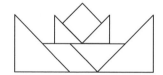

Storyteller 6: When Possum returned home, he had no light and all the fur was burned off his tail. To this day, Possum's tail is still bare. Owl called another meeting. He said, "We need someone else to go to The Land of the Sun People and bring back the light." He called,

Tangram: (Possum with long tail)

Chorus: Who, who, who will go?

Storyteller 7: Eagle stepped forward and said, "I will go. I will go to The Land of the Sun People and bring back the light. I can carry the light on top of my head as I fly home." So the animals agreed, and Eagle set off for The Land of the Sun People.

Tangram: (Eagle)

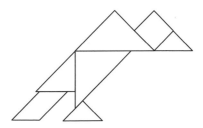

Chorus: He journeyed long, he traveled far.
               Until he came to a place as bright as a star.
               A place that was protected by guards.

Tangram: (Flying eagle)

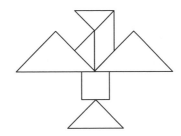

Storyteller 8:   When the guards were not looking, Eagle flew and snatched a piece of the light. He carried it
                  on top of his feathery head and began traveling home. He was nearly home when he felt

Chorus: A tickle, a tingle, a sizzle, a singe!
               Eagle's fine feathery head was on fire!

Tangram: (Fire)

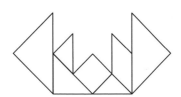

Storyteller 9:   When Eagle returned home, he had no light and all the feathers were burned off his head. To
                  this day, Eagle's head is still bare and we call him the "Bald Eagle." Owl called another meet-
                  ing. He said, "We need someone else to go to The Land of the Sun People and bring back the
                  light." He called,

Chorus: Who, who, who will go?

Storyteller 10:   Grandmother Spider stepped forward and said, "I will go. I will go to The Land of the Sun
                  People and bring back the light. I can carry the light on my back as I travel home." Owl said,

Grandmother Spider (Page 4)

"I mean no disrespect, Grandmother Spider, but you are so small." Grandmother Spider said, "Where there is a will, there is a way." So the animals agreed, and Grandmother Spider set off for The Land of the Sun People.

Tangram: (Spider)

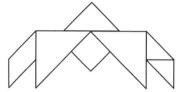

Storyteller 11:   About halfway into her journey, Grandmother Spider stopped and dug a hole in the rich earth. From the clay, she molded a small pot with a lid. She placed the pot on her back and traveled on.

Chorus: She journeyed long, she traveled far.
                  Until she came to a place as bright as a star.
                  A place that was protected by guards.

Tangram: (Pot)

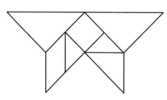

Storyteller 12:   Grandmother Spider was so small that the guards did not notice her. She gently took a piece of the light and placed it inside the clay pot. She carried it on top of her back and began traveling home. She was nearly home when she felt

Chorus: A tickle, a tingle, a sizzle, a singe!
                  The clay pot was full of fire!

Tangram: (Fire)

Storyteller 13:   Grandmother Spider took the hot pot and hurled it into the air. It exploded in fiery brilliance. There in the sky hung this great ball of light that today we call the sun. Grandmother Spider was a hero! Because she brought light to the animals of the northern lands, she was greatly honored. If you look at Grandmother Spider's web, it is in the shape of the rays of the sun. And to this day, you can still hear Grandmother Spider saying, "Where there is a will, there is a way."

Tangram: (Sun)

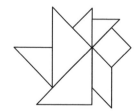

The Greedy Frog
Australia

Storyteller 1: In the time of dreaming, there lived a GIGANTIC frog. He was nearly as big as a mountain! After Rainbow Serpent came down from the sky to create the earth, mountains rose, valleys formed, and water appeared in every form. There were rivers, billabongs, lakes, and ponds. The land was beautiful, and all the animals shared the water.

Tangram: (Frog)

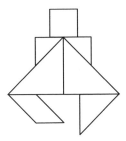

Storyteller 2: One day the gigantic frog became very thirsty. So he hopped over to the rivers and he drank all the water—SLURP! He was still thirsty, so he hopped over to the billabongs and he drank all the water—SLURP! He was still thirsty, so he hopped over to the lakes and he drank all the water—SLURP! Can you believe he was still thirsty? So he hopped over to the ponds and he drank all the water—SLURP!

Tangram: (River)

Storyteller 3: When he was finished, guess how much water was left? That's right! None! The gigantic frog was a greedy frog! He drank all the water in Australia! The water had filled his gigantic belly, making it big and round. He could hardly move. He became so tired that he fell into a deep sleep.

Storyteller 4: Now the land was without water. The river beds were cracked, the billabongs were parched, the lakes were dusty, and the ponds were dry. Because there was no water, terrible things happened to the land. The trees sagged, the leaves fell, and the flowers wilted.

Tangram: (Tree)

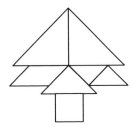

From *Tangram Tales: Story Theater Using the Ancient Chinese Puzzle* by Dianne de Las Casas. Westport, CT: Teacher Ideas Press. Copyright © 2009.

The Greedy Frog (Page 2)

Storyteller 5: The animals were so thirsty, they could barely move. With all their strength, they came together to discuss their troubles. Kangaroos, wallabies, koalas, dingoes, wombats, kookaburras, emus, and eels gathered. Kangaroo said, "Perhaps we can talk to the greedy frog and ask for our water back." One by one, the animals tried to talk to the greedy frog, but still he slept.

Tangram: (Kangaroo)

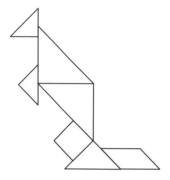

Storyteller 6: Koala said, "We have to do something soon! We cannot live without water!" Dingo said, "Let us force the water out of him by jumping on him."

Tangram: (Bear)

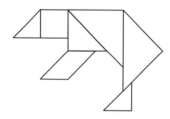

Chorus: The animals jumped and jumped and jumped.
But still the greedy frog slept (snore).

Storyteller 7: Emu said, "I have an idea. Let us force the water out of him by dancing on him."

Tangram: (Emu)

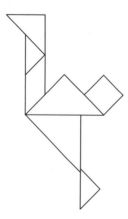

The Greedy Frog (Page 3)

Chorus: The animals danced and danced and danced.
But still the greedy frog slept (snore).

Storyteller 8: Then Eel said, "Let us force the water out of him by tickling him. Once he starts laughing, his belly will shake and the water will pour out."

Tangram: (Eel)

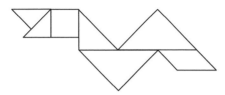

Chorus: The animals tickled and tickled and tickled and . . .

Storyteller 9: The greedy frog began to quiver and quake. Then he began to shiver and shake. His belly began to wiggle and jiggle. Suddenly, he burst out laughing. The animals ran for cover as the water spilled out. The waters ran into the river beds. The waters rushed into the billabongs. The waters tumbled into the lakes. And the waters poured into the ponds.

Storyteller 10: Once again, water had returned to Australia, and the animals were able to share the water. Again, the trees stood tall, the leaves danced in the wind, and the flowers lifted their faces to the warm sun. The once-gigantic frog shrank and shrank and shrank until he was no bigger than the size of your hand. The earth was beautiful once more.

Tangram: (Flower)

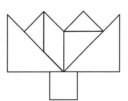

Storyteller 11: From that time on, the animals agreed to take no more than their share of the water. Everyone, that is, except for the greedy frog. To this day, greedy frogs still live in Australia. The Aborigines know that when the frogs fill their bellies up with water and bury themselves deep beneath the earth, it is a warning that a drought is coming.

Tangram: (Frog)

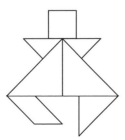

Chorus: And that is the tale of the greedy frog.

Henny Penny
England

Storyteller 1: One day Henny Penny was clucking along when an acorn fell on her head. "Ouch!" she yelled. She reached up and felt a lump. When she looked up, she saw the sky. She cried,

Chorus: The sky is falling! The sky is falling! It's a terrible thing!
Hurry up! Hurry up! I must go tell the king!

Tangram: (Hen)

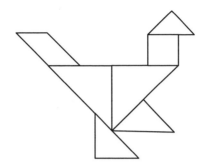

Storyteller 2: Along the way, Henny Penny met Rooster Looster. Rooster Looster asked, "Where are you going?" Henny Penny cried,

Chorus: The sky is falling! The sky is falling! It's a terrible thing!
Hurry up! Hurry up! I must go tell the king!

Tangram: (Rooster)

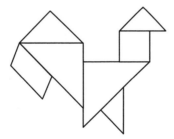

Storyteller 3: Along the way, Henny Penny and Rooster Looster met Ducky Lucky. Ducky Lucky asked, "Where are you going?" They cried,

Chorus: The sky is falling! The sky is falling! It's a terrible thing!
Hurry up! Hurry up! We must go tell the king!

Tangram: (Duck)

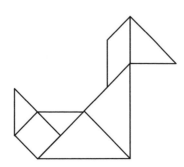

From *Tangram Tales: Story Theater Using the Ancient Chinese Puzzle* by Dianne de Las Casas. Westport, CT: Teacher Ideas Press. Copyright © 2009.

Storyteller 4:   Along the way, Henny Penny, Rooster Looster, and Ducky Lucky met Goosey Loosey. Goosey Loosey asked, "Where are you going?" They cried,

Chorus: The sky is falling! The sky is falling! It's a terrible thing! Hurry up! Hurry up! We must go tell the king!

Tangram: (Goose)

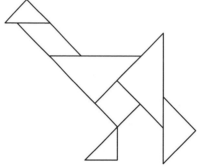

Storyteller 5:   Along the way, Henny Penny, Rooster Looster, Ducky Lucky, and Goosey Loosey met Turkey Lurkey. Turkey Lurkey asked, "Where are you going?" They cried,

Chorus: The sky is falling! The sky is falling! It's a terrible thing! Hurry up! Hurry up! We must go tell the king!

Tangram: (Turkey)

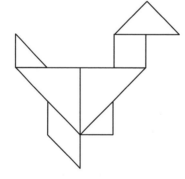

Storyteller 6:   Along the way, Henny Penny, Rooster Looster, Ducky Lucky, Goosey Loosey, and Turkey Lurkey met Foxy Loxy. Foxy Loxy asked, "Where are you going?" They cried,

Chorus: The sky is falling! The sky is falling! It's a terrible thing! Hurry up! Hurry up! We must go tell the king!

Tangram: (Fox sitting)

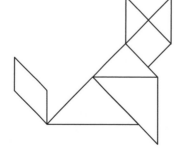

Storyteller 7: Foxy Loxy's stomach grumbled and he licked his lips. "Dinner!" he thought to himself. Foxy Loxy said, "That is not the way to the king. I will show you the way. Follow me." So Henny Penny, Rooster Looster, Ducky Lucky, Goosey Loosey, and Turkey Lurkey followed Foxy Loxy.

Tangram: (Fox walking)

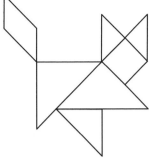

Storyteller 8: Henny Penny, Rooster Looster, Ducky Lucky, Goosey Loosey, and Turkey Lurkey followed Foxy Loxy to a dark cave. Foxy Loxy said, "The king is in there." So everyone walked into the cave. Henny Penny said, "I don't see the king." Foxy Loxy said, licking his lips, "I am the king now, and I am about to have my royal dinner!" Just then, they heard loud barking nearby.

Chorus: [Bark.]

Tangram: (Dog running)

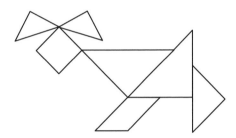

Storyteller 9: It was the king's hound dog. Foxy Loxy ran out of the cave with the dog chasing close behind. Henny Penny, Rooster Looster, Ducky Lucky, Goosey Loosey, and Turkey Lurkey escaped and ran back home. From that time on, Henny Penny decided that if the sky ever fell again, she would keep it to herself!

Tangram: (Hen)

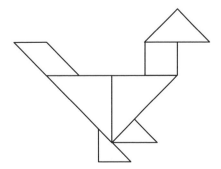

Chorus: The sky is falling! The sky is falling! It's a terrible thing!
Shhh. Be quiet. Shhh. Be quiet. I won't go tell the king!

The Hodja's Bet
Turkey

Storyteller 1:   On a cold, shivery night as the snow piled high, a group of men decided to visit the Hodja, the village's wise man. They were hungry and wanted to trick the Hodja into giving them a warm meal. They knocked on the door of the Hodja's house.

Tangram: (House)

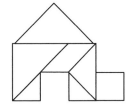

Storyteller 2:   The Hodja answered and asked, "What can I do for you, my friends?" The men answered, "We would like to have a bet with you, Hodja. If you win, we feed you a bowl full of food. If we win, you feed us a bowl full of food." The Hodja considered the idea and agreed.

Tangram: (Bowl)

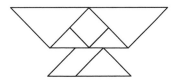

Storyteller 3:   The Hodja asked, "What is the bet?" One of the men said, "You must stay in the village square by the cemetery all night. You cannot eat, and even if it is snowing, you cannot have a fire."

Tangram: (Fire)

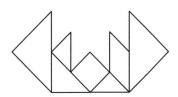

The Hodja's Bet (page 2)

Storyteller 4: The Hodja liked a good challenge. "Agreed," he said. That night, the Hodja bundled up in his warmest clothing and coat and walked to the village square by the cemetery. The men watched as the Hodja made himself comfortable.

Tangram: (Man sitting)

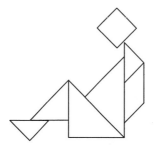

Storyteller 5: As the night wore on, the Hodja became spooked. First he heard the wind . . .

Chorus: Wooooooooooooooooo. Wooooooooooooooooooo.

Storyteller 5: And thought it might be a ghost!

Tangram: (Ghost figure)

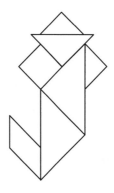

Storyteller 6: Then the Hodja heard a pack of wolves howling . . .

Chorus: Arooooooooooooooo! Arooooooooooooooooo!

Tangram: (Two dogs)

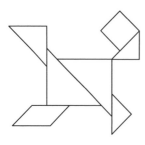 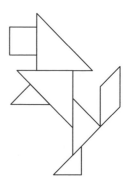

Storyteller 6:   And thought they might be out to get him!

Storyteller 7:   Then the Hodja caught sight of a single candle burning in a distant house window. The candle's bright flame comforted him, and he began to feel warmth. His fears began to disappear.

Tangram: (Candle)

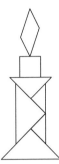

Storyteller 8:   In the morning, the men came to the square. They found the Hodja alive and well. "How did you survive the night?" they asked. The Hodja said, "At first, I was spooked by a ghostly wind. Then I heard the horrible howling of a pack of wolves. Finally, I saw a candle in a distant house window and it comforted me."

Tangram: (Candle)

Storyteller 9:   One of the men cried, "Hodja! You cheated! You lost the bet. You were not supposed to have a fire." The Hodja replied, "How is a distant candle a fire? I couldn't even feel its warmth!" But the men insisted that the Hodja had cheated. The Hodja gave in and promised to fulfill the bet, giving them each a bowl full of food the next day.

The Hodja's Bet (page 4)

Storyteller 10: The next day, the men came over for their meal. They waited and waited until their stomachs grumbled with hunger. "Where is the Hodja?" they cried. When they searched for him, they found him outside next to a pot hanging from a tree. Underneath, a candle burned.

Tangram: (Pot and candle underneath)

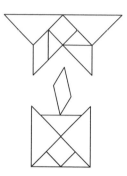

Storyteller 11: The men said, "Hodja, that is not cooking! How do you think the flame from a small candle is enough fire to cook an entire meal?" The Hodja smiled and said, "Yesterday, you said a candle's flame was a fire. Either you are right or I am right. Now who is the cheater, you or me?" The men hung their heads. The Hodja was right. He had rightfully won the bet.

Storyteller 12: The next night, the men fulfilled their end of the bargain. The Hodja and his friends shared a delicious meal by the light of a single candle.

Tangram: (Candle)

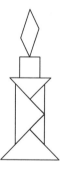

Chorus: The Hodja is a very wise man.
             If anyone can win a bet, the Hodja can!

From *Tangram Tales: Story Theater Using the Ancient Chinese Puzzle* by Dianne de Las Casas. Westport, CT: Teacher Ideas Press. Copyright © 2009.

The House That Jack Built
Mother Goose

Chorus: This is the house that Jack built.

Tangram: (House)

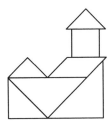

Storyteller 1:   This is the malt

Chorus: That lay in the house that Jack built.

Tangram: (Goblet)

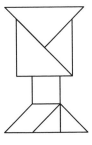

Storyteller 1:   This is the rat
               That ate the malt

Chorus: That lay in the house that Jack built.

Tangram: (Rat)

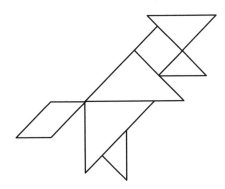

Storyteller 2:   This is the cat
That chased the rat
That ate the malt

Chorus: That lay in the house that Jack built.

Tangram: (Cat)

Storyteller 3:   This is the dog
That worried the cat
That chased the rat
That ate the malt

Chorus: That lay in the house that Jack built.

Tangram: (Dog)

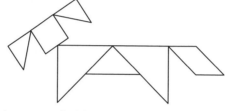

Storyteller 4:   This is the cow with the crumpled horn
That tossed the dog
That worried the cat
That chased the rat
That ate the malt

Chorus: That lay in the house that Jack built.

Tangram: (Cow with horn)

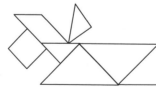

Storyteller 5:   This is the maiden all forlorn
That milked the cow with the crumpled horn
That tossed the dog
That worried the cat
That chased the rat
That ate the malt

Chorus: That lay in the house that Jack built.

Tangram: (Maiden)

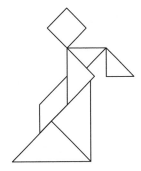

Storyteller 5: This is the man all tattered and torn
                That kissed the maiden all forlorn
                That milked the cow with the crumpled horn
                That tossed the dog
                That worried the cat
                That chased the rat
                That ate the malt

Chorus: That lay in the house that Jack built.

Tangram: (Man)

Storyteller 6: This is the priest all shaven and shorn
                That married the man all tattered and torn
                That kissed the maiden all forlorn
                That milked the cow with the crumpled horn
                That tossed the dog
                That worried the cat
                That chased the rat
                That ate the malt

Chorus: That lay in the house that Jack built.

The House That Jack Built

Tangram: (Man praying)

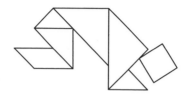

Storyteller 7:   This is the rooster that crowed in the morn
                  That waked the priest all shaven and shorn
                  That married the man all tattered and torn
                  That kissed the maiden all forlorn
                  That milked the cow with the crumpled horn
                  That tossed the dog
                  That worried the cat
                  That chased the rat
                  That ate the malt

Chorus: That lay in the house that Jack built.

Tangram: (Rooster)

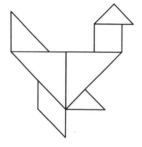

Storyteller 8:   This is the farmer sowing his corn
                  That kept the rooster that crowed in the morn
                  That waked the priest all shaven and shorn
                  That married the man all tattered and torn
                  That kissed the maiden all forlorn
                  That milked the cow with the crumpled horn
                  That tossed the dog
                  That worried the cat
                  That chased the rat
                  That ate the malt

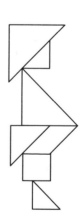

Chorus: That lay in the house that Jack built.

Tangram: (Farmer)

The Fox's Daughter
China

Storyteller 1: Long ago in the land of fiery red dragons there lived a beautiful girl named Feng-Lien. She was quite lucky, for she was born the daughter of a fox. Foxes have magical powers. A fox's child knows just as much magic and can take human form.

Tangram: (Fox)

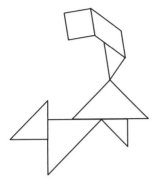

Storyteller 2: One day, a young, lazy student named Liu was boating when he should have been studying. He saw the form of a beautiful girl dancing in the reeds. He quickly docked his boat and tied it to a willow tree. He jumped out of the boat and began searching for the girl.

Tangram: (Man in boat)

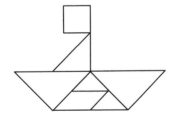

Storyteller 3: He heard mocking laughter and tried to follow its sound. He ran in all directions, first tearing his silk robe and then breaking a sandal strap. At last, he found the girl leaning against a tree. She was so beautiful that she took his breath away.

Tangram: (Standing girl)

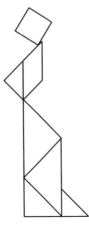

The Fox's Daughter (Page 2)

Storyteller 4: The girl spoke, "If only Master Liu studied as hard as he chased me, he would earn a high place in the Examination Hall." Liu asked her name and how she knew so much about him. She answered, "My name is Feng-Lien, and that is all I will tell you. I must go now."

Tangram: (Man and woman talking)

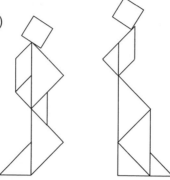

Storyteller 5: Liu cried, "No, please don't go! Please tell me where we shall meet again." Feng-Lien said, "Look for me in your books." Then she took out a gilded silver mirror and gave it to Liu. The beautiful fox maiden said, "You may see my reflection in the mirror but only through your books." In a moment, she vanished, saying,

Chorus: If you wish to see my face,
You must look in the right place.

Tangram: (Mirror)

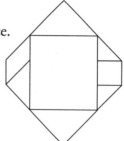

Storyteller 6: Liu was puzzled, but he went home with his gift. Each time he looked into the mirror, he only saw the back of Feng-Lien. When he went to his room, he remembered Feng-Lien's words.
Chorus: If you wish to see my face,
You must look in the right place.

Storyteller 7: He pulled out his books and looked inside, but he did not see Feng-Lien's face. Frustrated, he began studying in earnest. He discovered that when he studied and read, he saw Feng-Lien's pretty face in the mirror, smiling and nodding. "Ah!" cried Liu, "That is what she meant!"

Tangram: (Man reading book)

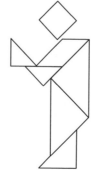

The Fox's Daughter

Storyteller 8:   For more than a month, Liu did nothing but study and study. He buried himself in his books. Each time he looked into the mirror, Feng-Lien smiled, pleased.

Tangram: (Man with book)

Storyteller 9:   Then summer came and the fine weather beckoned him. He put down the books and went boating once more. When he returned home, he looked into the mirror and Feng-Lien's back was to him. She was not pleased! Liu had forgotten her words.

Chorus: If you wish to see my face,
You must look in the right place.

Tangram: (Man boating)

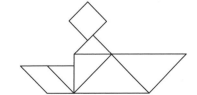

Storyteller 10:   One day, friends came by and asked him to go fishing. Happily, Liu agreed even though in his heart he knew he would not see Feng-Lien's face if he went. He was out all night. When he came back, he looked in the mirror. It was empty. Feng-Lien had disappeared.

Tangram: (Mirror)

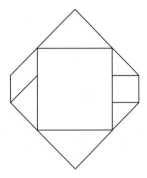

From *Tangram Tales: Story Theater Using the Ancient Chinese Puzzle* by Dianne de Las Casas. Westport, CT: Teacher Ideas Press. Copyright © 2009.

Storyteller 11: "Oh no!" cried Liu. He then dedicated himself to his books. Day and night, he did nothing but study and read. He studied until the day came to go to the Examination Hall. Liu took his tests and did so well that he took top honors.

Tangram: (Man with book)

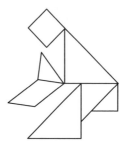

Storyteller 12: When Liu returned home, he looked in the mirror. Sure enough, beautiful Feng-Lien was there smiling at him. Suddenly, the mirror melted and the real Feng-Lien appeared before Liu. She said, "You have proven yourself a worthy man. A man of knowledge is most powerful of all." Feng-Lien and Liu were married. And all because Liu studied hard and remembered Feng-Lien's words.

Chorus: If you wish to see my face,
You must look in the right place.

Tangram: (Man and woman married)

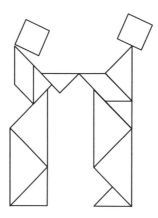

Storyteller 13: Liu became one of the most powerful men in China. As for Feng-Lien, she no longer had to use magic to keep Liu in line. All she had to do was give him a look and she could always outfox him.

From *Tangram Tales: Story Theater Using the Ancient Chinese Puzzle* by Dianne de Las Casas. Westport, CT: Teacher Ideas Press. Copyright © 2009.

It Could Always Be Worse!
Yiddish

Storyteller 1: A great while ago in a small village was a man who lived in a small house with his wife and seven children. It was crowded and noisy. Wanting peace, the man went to seek the wise counsel of the Rabbi.

Tangram: (Wise man)

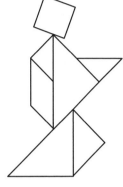

Storyteller 2: The man said, "Rabbi, my life is so miserable. I am in a small house with my wife and our seven children. It is always crowded and noisy. What should I do?" The Rabbi said,

Chorus: It could always be worse!

Storyteller 2: Then the Rabbi said, "Get a dog." So the man got a dog. The wife whined, the children cried, and the dog barked.

Chorus: Woof, woof, woof.

Tangram: (Dog)

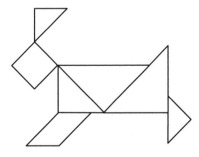

Storyteller 3: The man went back to the Rabbi and said, "Rabbi, my life is so miserable. I am in a small house with my wife, our seven children, and a barking dog. It is always crowded and noisy. What should I do?" The Rabbi said,

Chorus: It could always be worse!

Storyteller 3: Then the Rabbi said, "Get a cat." So the man got a cat. The wife whined, the children cried, the dog barked, and the cat meowed.

From *Tangram Tales: Story Theater Using the Ancient Chinese Puzzle* by Dianne de Las Casas. Westport, CT: Teacher Ideas Press. Copyright © 2009.

Chorus: Meow, meow, meow.

Tangram: (Cat)

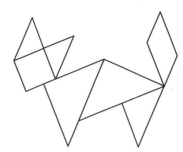

Storyteller 4:   The man went back to the Rabbi and said, "Rabbi, my life is so miserable. I am in a small house with my wife, our seven children, a barking dog, and a meowing cat. It is always crowded and noisy. What should I do?" The Rabbi said,

Chorus: It could always be worse!

Storyteller 5:   Then the Rabbi said, "Get a goose." So the man got a goose. The wife whined, the children cried, the dog barked, the cat meowed, and the goose honked.

Chorus: Honk, Honk, Honk.

Tangram: (Goose)

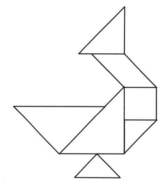

Storyteller 6:   The man went back to the Rabbi and said, "Rabbi, my life is so miserable. I am in a small house with my wife, our seven children, a barking dog, a meowing cat, and a honking goose. It is always crowded and noisy. What should I do?" The Rabbi said,

Chorus: It could always be worse!

Storyteller 7:   Then the Rabbi said, "Get a goat." So the man got a goat. The wife whined, the children cried, the dog barked, the cat meowed, the goose honked, and the goat bleated.

Chorus: Beeeh, Beeeh, Beeeh.

Tangram: (Goat)

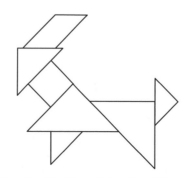

Storyteller 8: The man went back to the Rabbi and said, "Rabbi, my life is so miserable. I am in a small house with my wife, our seven children, a barking dog, a meowing cat, a honking goose, and a bleating goat. It is always crowded and noisy. What should I do?" The Rabbi said,

Chorus: It could always be worse!

Storyteller 9: Then the Rabbi said, "Get a pig." So the man got a pig. The wife whined, the children cried, the dog barked, the cat meowed, the goose honked, the goat bleated, and the pig oinked.

Chorus: Oink, oink, oink.

Tangram: (Pig)

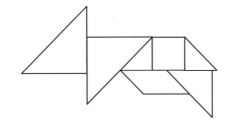

Storyteller 10: The man went back to the Rabbi and said, "Rabbi, my life is so miserable. I am in a small house with my wife, our seven children, a barking dog, a meowing cat, a honking goose, a bleating goat, and an oinking pig. It is always crowded and noisy. What should I do?" The Rabbi said,

Chorus: It could always be worse!

Storyteller 11: Then the Rabbi said, "Get a horse." So the man got a horse. The wife whined, the children cried, the dog barked, the cat meowed, the goose honked, the goat bleated, the pig oinked, and the horse neighed.

Chorus: [Neigh like a horse three times.]

Tangram: (Horse)

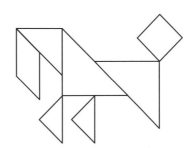

Storyteller 12: The man went back to the Rabbi and said, "Rabbi, my life is so miserable. I am in a small house with my wife, our seven children, a barking dog, a meowing cat, a honking goose, a bleating goat, an oinking pig, and a neighing horse. It is always crowded and noisy. What should I do?" The Rabbi said,

Chorus: It could always be worse!

Storyteller 13: Then the Rabbi said, "Get a cow." So the man got a cow. The wife whined, the children cried, the dog barked, the cat meowed, the goose honked, the goat bleated, the pig oinked, the horse neighed, and the cow mooed.

Chorus: Moo, moo, moo.

Tangram: (Cow)

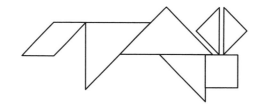

Storyteller 14: The man went back to the Rabbi and said, "I can't take it anymore! Rabbi, my life is so miserable. I am in a small house with my wife, our seven children, a barking dog, a meowing cat, a honking goose, a bleating goat, an oinking pig, a neighing horse, and a mooing cow. It is always crowded and noisy. What should I do?" The Rabbi said,

Chorus: It could always be worse!

Storyteller 15: Then the Rabbi said, "Get a job." So the man did. He's now a crossing guard at a school, where it is much quieter. The end.

Tangram: (Crossing guard)

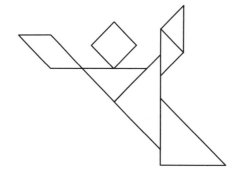

Jack Seeks His Fortune
Ireland

Storyteller 1: In a land of green rolling hills, there once lived a boy named Jack. One day, Jack decided that it was time for him to make his fortune. He began traveling down the road. He had not gone very far when he met a sad old donkey. The donkey said,

Chorus: Hee haw, I don't know what to do.
My master doesn't want me—can I go with you?

Tangram: (Donkey)

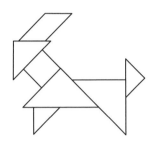

Storyteller 2: Jack said, "Sure!" And off the two traveled. They journeyed down the road a little ways when they met a sad old cow. The cow said,

Chorus: Moo moo, I don't know what to do.
My master doesn't want me—can I go with you?

Tangram: (Cow)

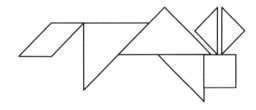

Storyteller 3: Jack said, "Sure!" And off the three traveled. They journeyed down the road a little ways when they met a sad old dog. The dog said,

Chorus: Arf arf, I don't know what to do.
My master doesn't want me—can I go with you?

Tangram: (Dog)

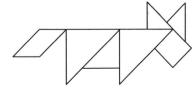

Storyteller 4: Jack said, "Sure!" And off the four traveled. They journeyed down the road a little ways when they met a sad old cat. The cat said,

Chorus: Meow meow, I don't know what to do.
My master doesn't want me—can I go with you?

Tangram: (Cat)

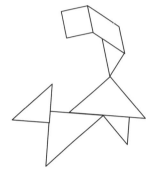

Storyteller 5: Jack said, "Sure!" And off the five traveled. They journeyed down the road a little ways when they met a sad old rooster. The rooster said,

Chorus: Cock-a-doodle-doo, I don't know what to do.
My master doesn't want me—can I go with you?

Tangram: (Rooster)

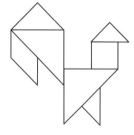

Storyteller 6: Jack said, "Sure!" And off they all traveled. They journeyed until it was nearly dark. Then Jack spotted a house. He told the animals, "Ssssshhhh" as he peeked in through the window. Much to his surprise, he saw a gang of robbers counting their gold!

Storyteller 7: Jack had a bright idea. He said, "When I wave my hand, make as much noise as you can." When the animals were ready, Jack gave the signal. The donkey brayed, the cow mooed, the dog barked, the cat meowed, and the rooster crowed. Together, they made such an awful racket that the noise scared away the robbers and they left behind all of their—gold!

Tangram: (Bag of gold)

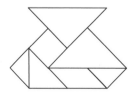

Jack Seeks His Fortune (Page 3)

Storyteller 8: Jack and the animals went inside the house and got comfortable. Then Jack began to worry that the robbers would come back. So he came up with another plan. He put the donkey near the door, the cow by the fireplace, the dog under the table, the cat in the rocking chair, and the rooster on a beam at the top. Finally, Jack fell asleep.

Tangram: (Bed)

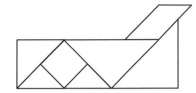

Storyteller 9: Jack was right. The robbers returned. They decided to look for their gold. They sent one of their men inside the house. When the robber came in, the rooster crowed loudly, the cat scratched him, the dog bit his leg, the cow slapped him with his tail, and the donkey kicked him out the door. He ran back to the other robbers, and they never returned to the house again.

Tangram: (Man running)

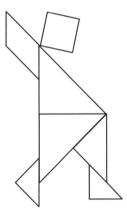

Storyteller 10: Jack and the animals had themselves a nice house and a big pile of—gold! They lived there in peace and contentment for the rest of their days. Jack made his fortune, but the best fortune of all was his friends.

Chorus: Hooray! Hooray! We know what to do . . .
We found our fortune; now we'll live with you!

Tangram: (House)

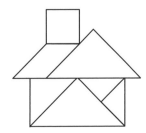

La Cucarachita Martina
Cuba

Storyteller 1:   La Señorita Cucarachita Martina vivía en una casita chiquita. Miss Martina Cockroach lived in a little house. She was sweeping her porch to some sassy salsa music. Around and around she danced. As she was dancing around, she looked down and noticed something shiny on the ground. It was a gold coin!

Tangram: (Woman dancing)

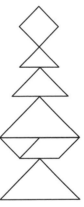

Storyteller 2:   "Ay yi yi!" la Señorita Cucarachita Martina cried. "I have good luck! What will I buy with this? Should I buy candies? Eh, no. Shoes? Eh, no. I want to buy . . . perfume so that I can smell *heavenly*."

Tangram: (Perfume bottle)

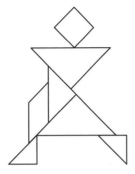

Storyteller 3:   So la Señorita Cucarachita Martina bought some perfume and wore it the next day. She was sitting on the veranda when along came Señor Torrito, Mr. Bull. Señor Torrito said,

Tangram: (Bull)

Chorus: Cucarachita Martina, you smell heavenly.
Will you please, will you please marry me?

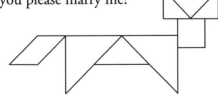

From *Tangram Tales: Story Theater Using the Ancient Chinese Puzzle* by Dianne de Las Casas. Westport, CT: Teacher Ideas Press. Copyright © 2009.

Storyteller 4: La Señorita Cucarachita Martina answered, "Señor Torrito, in the morning, how will you greet me?"

Chorus: ¡Mooooooooooo, moooooooooooo!

Storyteller 5: "¡Ay, no! That would frighten me!" So Señor Torrito went on his way. A little while later, Señor Gallito, Mr. Rooster, came by. Señor Gallito said,

Tangram: (Rooster)

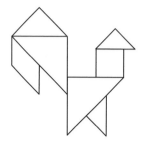

Chorus: Cucarachita Martina, you smell heavenly.
Will you please, will you please marry me?

Storyteller 6: La Señorita Cucarachita Martina answered, "Señor Gallito, in the morning, how will you greet me?"

Chorus: ¡Quiquiriqui, quiquiriqui!

Storyteller 7: "¡Ay, no! That would frighten me!" So Señor Gallito went on his way. A little while later, Señor Perrito, Mr. Dog, came by. Señor Perrito said,

Tangram: (Dog)

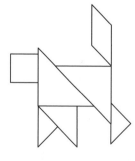

Chorus: Cucarachita Martina, you smell heavenly.
Will you please, will you please marry me?

Storyteller 8: La Señorita Cucarachita Martina answered, "Señor Perrito, in the morning, how will you greet me?"

Chorus: ¡Gua gua gua!

From Tangram Tales: Story Theater Using the Ancient Chinese Puzzle by Dianne de Las Casas. Westport, CT: Teacher Ideas Press. Copyright © 2009.

Storyteller 9: "¡Ay, no! That would frighten me!" So Señor Perrito went on his way. A little while later, Señor Chivito, Mr. Goat, came by. Señor Chivito said,

Tangram: (Goat)

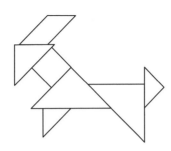

Chorus: Cucarachita Martina, you smell heavenly.
Will you please, will you please marry me?

Storyteller 10: La Señorita Cucarachita Martina answered, "Señor Chivito, in the morning, how will you greet me?"

Chorus: ¡Beeeh beeeh!

Storyteller 11: "¡Ay, no! That would frighten me!" So Señor Chivito went on his way. A little while later, Señor Ratoncito, Mr. Mouse, came by. Señor Ratoncito said,

Tangram: (Mouse)

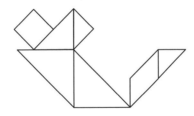

Chorus: Cucarachita Martina, you smell heavenly.
Will you please, will you please marry me?

Storyteller 12: La Señorita Cucarachita Martina answered, "Señor Ratoncito, in the morning, how will you greet me?"
"Good morning, mi cucarachita linda—my beautiful little cockroach," said Señor Ratoncito.

Storyteller 13: "Ooh, I like your style. Yes, I will marry you!" So Miss Martina Cockroach and Mr. Mouse were married. She smelled heavenly, and they lived happily. To this day, las cucarachitas y los ratoncitos, the cockroaches and the mice, still get along. You may even see them running together en tu casita chiquita, in your little house. ¡El Fin! The end!

From Tangram Tales: Story Theater Using the Ancient Chinese Puzzle by Dianne de Las Casas. Westport, CT: Teacher Ideas Press. Copyright © 2009.

The Mitten
Ukraine

Storyteller 1: On a cold, wintery day, Alexander trudged through the forest to gather firewood. He wore brand new mittens that his grandmother knitted for him. "Don't lose them!" she said, before he left the house.

Tangram: (Boy carrying wood)

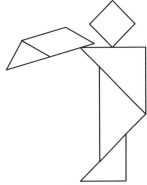

Storyteller 2: All morning, Alexander worked gathering wood until his sled was full. As he traveled back home, he didn't notice that he had dropped one of his mittens in the snow.

Tangram: (Mitten)

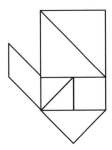

Storyteller 3: As soon as Alexander was out of sight, a little mouse scurried by. She was shivering with cold when she spied the mitten. She said, "Oh, this is the perfect place to keep warm!" She climbed inside.

Tangram: (Mouse)

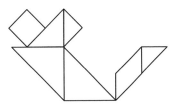

Storyteller 4: A little while later, a robin came hopping through the snow. He was shivering with cold when he spied the mitten. "This is the perfect place to keep warm!" He went to the mitten and asked, "Is there any room?" The mouse answered,

Chorus: There's always room for one more!

Tangram: (Bird—Robin)

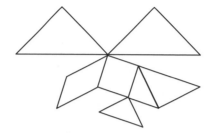

Storyteller 5: A little while later, a rabbit came hopping through the snow. He was shivering with cold when he spied the mitten. "This is the perfect place to keep warm!" He went to the mitten and asked, "Is there any room?" The mouse and the robin answered,

Chorus: There's always room for one more!

Tangram: (Rabbit)

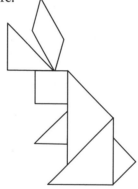

Storyteller 6: A little while later, a fox came romping through the snow. He was shivering with cold when he spied the mitten. "This is the perfect place to keep warm!" He went to the mitten and asked, "Is there any room?" The mouse, the robin, and the rabbit answered,

Chorus: There's always room for one more!

Tangram: (Fox)

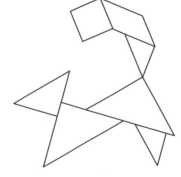

From *Tangram Tales: Story Theater Using the Ancient Chinese Puzzle* by Dianne de Las Casas. Westport, CT: Teacher Ideas Press. Copyright © 2009.

Storyteller 7: A little while later, a wolf came trotting through the snow. He was shivering with cold when he spied the mitten. "This is the perfect place to keep warm!" He went to the mitten and asked, "Is there any room?" It was getting pretty tight, but the mouse, the robin, the rabbit, and the fox answered,

Chorus: There's always room for one more!

Storyteller 8: A little while later, a wild boar came snorting through the snow. He was shivering with cold when he spied the mitten. "This is the perfect place to keep warm!" He went to the mitten and asked, "Is there any room?" It was getting super duper tight, but the mouse, the robin, the rabbit, the fox, and the wolf answered,

Chorus: There's always room for one more!

Tangram: (Wild boar)

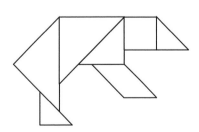

Storyteller 9: A little while later, a bear came blustering through the snow. He was shivering with cold when he spied the mitten. "This is the perfect place to keep warm!" He went to the mitten and asked, "Is there any room?" But the mitten was full! The mouse, the robin, the rabbit, the fox, the wolf, and the boar answered,

Chorus: There's no more room!

Tangram: (Bear)

Storyteller 10: But the bear said,

Chorus: There's always room for one more!

Storyteller 10: The bear crammed and jammed himself into the mitten. The mitten moaned and groaned as its seams heaved. Just then, a cricket hopped by. "This is the perfect place to keep warm. I'm so tiny, I'll just squeeze myself in." And so she tried. But alas, that was the cricket that broke the mitten's seams.

Storyteller 11: The mitten bulged and then burst!

Chorus: POP!

Tangram: (Mitten burst apart)

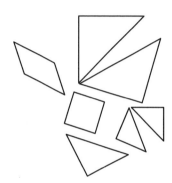

Storyteller 12: A short while later, Alexander came by looking for his lost mitten. All he found were some scraps of red wool and leather. "Oh well," said Alexander, "I am sure grandmother will have finished new mittens by now." On that cold and wintery day, Alexander hurried home to warm himself by the fire.

Tangram: (Boy hurrying)

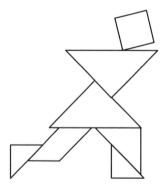

The Old Woman and Her Pig
England

Storyteller 1: One evening, an old woman went to market to buy a fat pig. On the way home, she came to a fence. The old woman said,

Chorus: I went to market to buy a fat pig (clap, clap).
Let's go home again—jiggedy jig (clap, clap).

Tangram: (Pig)

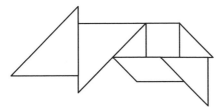

Storyteller 2: The old woman tried to get her pig to jump the fence, but it wouldn't. She saw a dog and said,

Chorus: I went to market to buy a fat pig (clap, clap).
Let's go home again—jiggedy jig (clap, clap).

Tangram: (Dog)

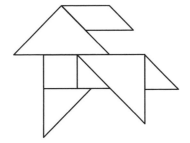

Storyteller 3: The old woman said, "Dog, nip the pig. Pig won't jump the fence, and I won't get home tonight!" But the dog would not. She saw a stick and said,

Chorus: I went to market to buy a fat pig (clap, clap).
Let's go home again—jiggedy jig (clap, clap).

Tangram: (Stick)

Storyteller 4: The old woman said, "Stick, poke the dog. Dog won't nip the pig. Pig won't jump the fence, and I won't get home tonight!" But the stick would not. She saw a fire and said,

Chorus: I went to market to buy a fat pig (clap, clap). Let's go home again—jiggedy jig (clap, clap).

Tangram: (Candle with fire)

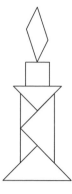

Storyteller 5: The old woman said, "Fire, burn the stick. Stick won't poke the dog. Dog won't nip the pig. Pig won't jump the fence, and I won't get home tonight!" But the fire would not. She saw some water and said,

Chorus: I went to market to buy a fat pig (clap, clap). Let's go home again—jiggedy jig (clap, clap).

Tangram: (Pitcher of water)

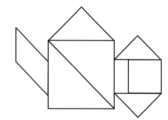

Storyteller 6: The old woman said, "Water, quench the fire. Fire won't burn the stick. Stick won't poke the dog. Dog won't nip the pig. Pig won't jump the fence, and I won't get home tonight!" But the water would not. She saw an ox and said,

Chorus: I went to market to buy a fat pig (clap, clap). Let's go home again—jiggedy jig (clap, clap).

Tangram: (Ox)

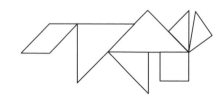

From *Tangram Tales: Story Theater Using the Ancient Chinese Puzzle* by Dianne de Las Casas. Westport, CT: Teacher Ideas Press. Copyright © 2009.

Storyteller 7: The old woman said, "Ox, drink the water. Water won't quench the fire. Fire won't burn the stick. Stick won't poke the dog. Dog won't nip the pig. Pig won't jump the fence, and I won't get home tonight!" But the ox would not. She saw a rope and said,

Chorus: I went to market to buy a fat pig (clap, clap).
Let's go home again—jiggedy jig (clap, clap).

Tangram: (Rope)

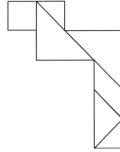

Storyteller 8: The old woman said, "Rope, lasso the ox. Ox won't drink the water. Water won't quench the fire. Fire won't burn the stick. Stick won't poke the dog. Dog won't nip the pig. Pig won't jump the fence, and I won't get home tonight!" But the rope would not. She saw a rat and said,

Chorus: I went to market to buy a fat pig (clap, clap).
Let's go home again—jiggedy jig (clap, clap).

Tangram: (Rat)

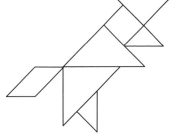

Storyteller 9: The old woman said, "Rat, gnaw the rope. Rope won't lasso the ox. Ox won't drink the water. Water won't quench the fire. Fire won't burn the stick. Stick won't poke the dog. Dog won't nip the pig. Pig won't jump the fence, and I won't get home tonight!" But the rat would not. She saw a cat and said,

Chorus: I went to market to buy a fat pig (clap, clap).
Let's go home again—jiggedy jig (clap, clap).

Tangram: (Cat)

Storyteller 10: The old woman said, "Cat, chase the rat. Rat won't gnaw the rope. Rope won't lasso the ox. Ox won't drink the water. Water won't quench the fire. Fire won't burn the stick. Stick won't poke the dog. Dog won't nip the pig. Pig won't jump the fence, and I won't get home tonight!" But the cat would not. The cat said, "If you go to the cow and give me milk, I will chase the rat."

Tangram: (Cat 2)

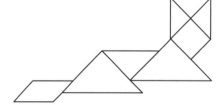

Storyteller 11: So the old woman went to the cow and said, "Please give me some milk." The cow said, "I will give you milk if you go to the barn and get me some hay."

Tangram: (Cow)

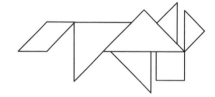

Storyteller 12: So the old woman went to the barn. Hey! Hey! Hey! The old woman gathered hay!

Tangram: (Barn)

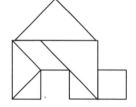

Storyteller 13: The old woman gave the hay to the cow. The cow gave her some milk. The old woman gave the milk to the cat. The cat began to chase the rat. The rat began to gnaw the rope. The rope began to lasso the ox. The ox began to drink the water. The water began to quench the fire. The fire began to burn the stick. The stick began to poke the dog. The dog began to nip the pig. The frightened pig jumped over the fence. And that's how the old woman got home that night.

Tangram: (House)

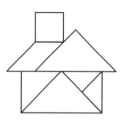

Chorus: I went to market to buy a fat pig (clap, clap).
Now I'm home again—jiggedy jig (clap, clap).

From Tangram Tales: Story Theater Using the Ancient Chinese Puzzle by Dianne de Las Casas. Westport, CT: Teacher Ideas Press. Copyright © 2009.

Rabbit's Turnip
China

Storyteller 1: In the snowy mountains of China, a rabbit stood beneath the gray sky and twitched his nose. More snow was on its way and he needed to find food.

Tangram: (Rabbit)

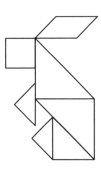

Storyteller 2: He hopped around, and after digging in the ground a while, a turnip turned up. A short while later, a second turnip turned up. Quickly, Rabbit rolled the two turnips home.

Tangram: (House)

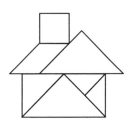

Storyteller 3: Once inside his cozy burrow, he nibbled at one of the turnips. His thoughts turned to his friend, Donkey. "I wonder if Donkey has found enough food. I have enough to eat. I should give her this extra turnip."

Chorus: To my friend's house I will go.
To give her a gift in the midst of the snow.

Tangram: (Donkey)

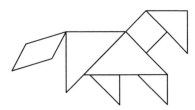

Storyteller 4: Rabbit took the turnip to Donkey's house and placed it in front of the door. When Donkey returned home with a potato, she found the surprise gift. Her thoughts turned to her friend, Goat. "I wonder if Goat has found enough food. I have enough to eat. I should give him this extra turnip."

Chorus: To my friend's house I will go.
To give him a gift in the midst of the snow.

Tangram: (Goat)

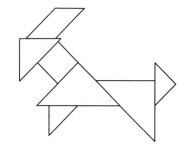

Storyteller 5: Donkey took the turnip to Goat's house and placed it in front of the door. When Goat returned home with a cabbage, he found the surprise gift. His thoughts turned to his friend, Deer. "I wonder if Deer has found enough food. I have enough to eat. I should give her this extra turnip."

Chorus: To my friend's house I will go.
To give her a gift in the midst of the snow.

Tangram: (Deer)

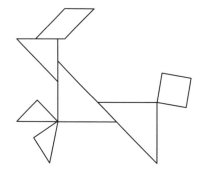

Storyteller 6: Goat took the turnip to Deer's house and placed it in front of the door. When Deer returned home with a carrot, she found the surprise gift. Her thoughts turned to her friend, Rabbit. "I wonder if Rabbit has found enough food. I have enough to eat. I should give him this extra turnip."

Chorus: To my friend's house I will go.
To give him a gift in the midst of the snow.

Rabbit's Turnip (Page 3)

Tangram: (Rabbit)

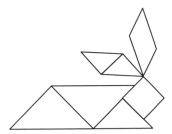

Storyteller 7:   When Rabbit awoke in the morning, he stepped outside. Imagine his surprise to see a turnip turn up! "Now what friend could have left me such a nice gift?" Because the drifts of snow covered all the tracks, Rabbit had no idea who it was. But Rabbit had an idea.

Storyteller 8:   He hopped around and invited all of his friends over for a big bowl of turnip soup. Rabbit, Donkey, Goat, and Deer shared the turnip that turned up.

Tangram: (Bowl)

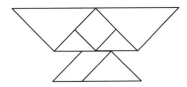

Chorus: A gift is definitely a delight to find.
    But to share it with your friends is truly divine.

Silly Ivan's Salt
Russia

Storyteller 1: Once, on the far side of yesterday, there was a young man called Ivan. He often did silly things, so his father and two older brothers called him Silly Ivan.

Chorus: Ivan, oh Ivan, you're so willy nilly.
Ivan, oh Ivan, you're just plain silly.

Tangram: (Dancing man)

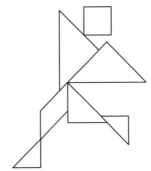

Storyteller 2: The day came for the brothers to seek their own fortune, so Ivan's father gave them beautiful ships laden with gold, jewels, and silks. Ivan said, "Father, I want to seek my fortune. May I have a ship too?"

Tangram: (Sailing ship)

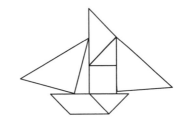

Storyteller 3: Ivan's father laughed. "Ivan, I cannot give you a ship laden with riches, for you are so silly that you will wreck the ship and squander the treasure." But Ivan was persistent, and finally his father gave in. He only gave Ivan a little ship with old sailormen. As Ivan sailed away, his mother cried out, "Ivan, be good. Don't be silly!"

Chorus: Ivan, oh Ivan, you're so willy nilly.
Ivan, oh Ivan, you're just plain silly.

Tangram: (Sailing ship)

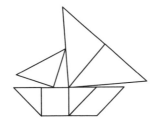

Silly Ivan's Salt (Page 2)

Storyteller 4: Ivan and his crew sailed for days. On the fifth day, a huge storm raged. The sea beat against the small ship, and the wind blew them to a deserted island. As soon as the ship landed, the sailors began repairing the ship and creating new sails with old rags, brocades, and embroidered shawls. Ivan, on the other hand, ran to explore the island. The sailors called out, "Stay with us, away from danger. Ivan, don't be silly!"

Chorus: Ivan, oh Ivan, you're so willy nilly.
Ivan, oh Ivan, you're just plain silly.

Tangram: (Man running)

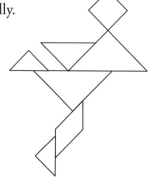

Storyteller 5: But of course, Ivan didn't listen, because he was . . . silly! Soon, he came to a tall mountain. There was green all around, but there was nothing on the mountain. The mountain was completely white, and Ivan thought it was snow. Because he was thirsty, Ivan put the white snow in his mouth. He discovered it was salt!

Tangram: (Mountain)

Storyteller 6: Ivan ran back to the ship. He cried out, "I have made the most wonderful discovery! Sailors, empty the ship and help me load as much salt as we can carry." The sailors did as they were told. When the ship was full, they set sail once again.

Tangram: (Sailing ship)

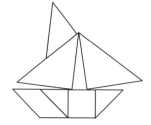

Silly Ivan's Salt (Page 3)

Storyteller 7: Some time later, Ivan and his crew docked in a small seaside village. Ivan made his way to the palace and asked to see the Tzar. The Tzar asked, "Who are you?" Ivan answered, "My name is Ivan, and I am selling salt!" The Tzar asked to see the salt. When Ivan showed the Tzar a goblet full of the white substance, the Tzar laughed. "You cannot sell this! This is nothing but white dust. You must be silly!"

Chorus: Ivan, oh Ivan, you're so willy nilly.
Ivan, oh Ivan, you're just plain silly.

Tangram: (Goblet)

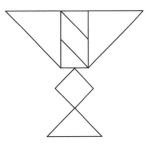

Storyteller 8: Ivan said, "Let me into the kitchen, and I will prove its worth." The Tzar agreed. So Ivan went into the kitchen. When the cook poured the soup into bowls, Ivan added a pinch of salt to each bowl.

Tangram: (Bowl)

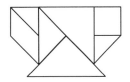

Storyteller 9: When the Tzar tasted the soup, he said, "I have never tasted anything so delicious! I will pay you whatever you desire for your salt." So Ivan charged the Tzar one bag of gold for every bag of salt. The Tzar's daughter, Katya, fell silly in love with Ivan, and Ivan fell silly in love with the princess. They married and sailed away together.

Chorus: Ivan, oh Ivan, you're so willy nilly.
Ivan, oh Ivan, you're just plain silly.

Tangram: (Sailing ship)

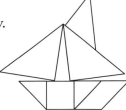

Storyteller 10: After sailing for some time, Ivan spotted two large ships. They happened to be the ships of Ivan's older brothers. When they met, Ivan's brothers became jealous of his riches and his beautiful bride. They said, "You are much too silly for all of this!" So they threw Ivan overboard.

Chorus: Ivan, oh Ivan, you're so willy nilly.
Ivan, oh Ivan, you're just plain silly.

Silly Ivan's Salt (Page 4)

Tangram: (Two sailing ships)

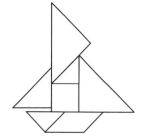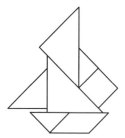

Storyteller 11:   Ivan swam until he came to an island. On this island was a huge house. Inside the huge house lived a giant! When the giant saw Ivan, he asked, "What troubles you?" Ivan shared his story. The giant said, "Sadly, there is more to the tale than you know. With my magic, I can see that your oldest brother will marry the princess tomorrow."

Tangram: (Princess)

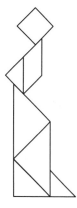

Storyteller 12:   Ivan said, "We must stop the wedding!" The giant agreed to help Ivan as long as Ivan promised not to boast of it. The giant put Ivan on his shoulders and waded through the sea, taking Ivan home.

Tangram: (House)

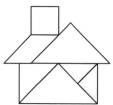

Storyteller 13:   When Ivan entered the house, the princess ran to him. "I am so glad you have returned!" They shared their tale with Ivan's father, and Ivan's father said, "Perhaps Ivan is not so silly after all." The oldest brother was angry and began bragging about his ability to wrestle a bear. Ivan, not to be outdone, said, "That is nothing! I rode on the shoulder of a giant to get here!" Suddenly, there was a great crash. The giant came thundering in.

Tangram: (Giant talking head)

Storyteller 14: The giant said, "I told you never to boast about me!" The giant was so angry that he began romping and stomping about, causing total destruction. When he was finished, Ivan said, "Look at what you have done! You have wrecked our home and ruined our feast. Shame on you!" The giant looked around and he was indeed ashamed. He said, "Ivan, you are right. I will never bother you again and you may boast of me for a thousand years." Then the giant left.

Tangram: (House)

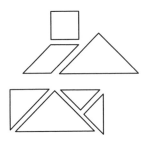

Storyteller 15: So Ivan became known far and wide as a brave, rich man who conquered a giant and married a princess. After that, no one dared to call Ivan silly even if he was still a bit silly.

Chorus: Ivan, oh Ivan, you're so willy nilly.
Ivan, oh Ivan, you're just plain silly!

Tangram: (Dancing man)

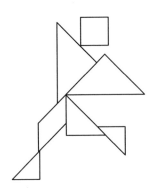

The Stonecutter
Japan

Storyteller 1:   There was once a stonecutter who chipped away slabs from the side of a great mountain. For a long time he was happy and asked for nothing more than what he had.

Tangram: (Mountain)

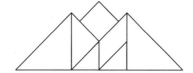

Storyteller 2:   One day as he was chipping away at the side of the mountain, he spied a beautiful house. He began to wish for a new life. He said, "Oh, if only I were a rich man, how happy I would be!"
The Great Mountain Spirit heard and said,

Chorus: What you wish is what you'll see.
A rich man is what you'll be.

Tangram: (Rich man)

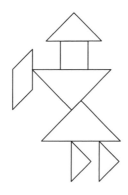

Storyteller 3:   When the stonecutter returned home, he found a splendid house with beautiful furniture. He soon forgot his old life as a stonecutter. One day as he was gazing out the window, he spied a handsome prince in a carriage. A gold umbrella was held over the prince's head to protect him from the sun. The stonecutter began to wish for a new life. He said, "Oh, if only I were a handsome prince, how happy I would be!"
The Great Mountain Spirit heard and said,

Chorus: What you wish is what you'll see.
A handsome prince is what you'll be.

Tangram: (Prince with umbrella)

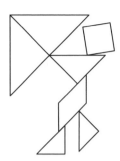

Storyteller 4:   The stonecutter became a handsome prince. He soon forgot his old life as a rich man. A gold umbrella was held over his head to protect him from the sun. One day as he was gazing around, he realized that the sun was more powerful than he. The stonecutter began to wish for a new life. He said, "Oh, if only I were a shining sun, how happy I would be!"
The Great Mountain Spirit heard and said,

Chorus: What you wish is what you'll see.
A shining sun is what you'll be.

Tangram: (Sun)

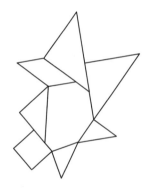

Storyteller 5:   The stonecutter became a shining sun. He soon forgot his old life as a handsome prince. He enjoyed his dominion in the sky. One day as he was gazing around, he realized that the cloud passing in front of him was more powerful than he. The stonecutter began to wish for a new life. He said, "Oh, if only I were a floating cloud, how happy I would be!"
The Great Mountain Spirit heard and said,

Chorus: What you wish is what you'll see.
A floating cloud is what you'll be.

Tangram: (Cloud)

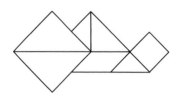

Storyteller 6: The stonecutter became a floating cloud. He soon forgot his old life as a shining sun. He floated freely across the sky. One day as he was gazing around, he realized that the immovable mountain in front of him was more powerful than he. The stonecutter began to wish for a new life. He said, "Oh, if only I were a tall mountain, how happy I would be!"
The Great Mountain Spirit heard and said,

Chorus: What you wish is what you'll see.
A tall mountain is what you'll be.

Tangram: (Mountain)

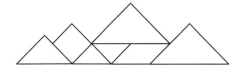

Storyteller 7: The stonecutter became a tall mountain. He soon forgot his old life as a floating cloud. He stood strong and immovable. One day as he was gazing around, he heard the chipping and clinking of falling stone. A stonecutter was carving into his side. He realized that the simple stonecutter was more powerful than he. The stonecutter began to wish for a new life. He said, "Oh, if only I were a stonecutter, how happy I would be!"
The Great Mountain Spirit heard and said,

Chorus: What you wish is what you'll see.
A stonecutter is what you'll be.

Tangram: (Stonecutter)

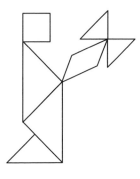

Storyteller 8: There was once a stonecutter who chipped away slabs from the side of a great mountain. From that time on, he was happy and asked for nothing more than what he had.

The Three Billy Goats Gruff
Norway

Storyteller 1: In the great mountains of Norway there lived three billy goats. Their names were the three Billy Goats Gruff. There was Little Billy Goat Gruff. There was Middle Billy Goat Gruff. And there was BIG Billy Goat Gruff.

Tangram: (Mountains)

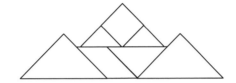

Storyteller 2: The three Billy Goats Gruff lived on one side of a river. Over that river was a bridge. Under that bridge lived a TROLL! No one dared to cross the bridge, because they were all afraid of the troll!

Tangram: (Troll)

Storyteller 3: One day, Little Billy Goat Gruff saw sweet green grass on the other side. He wanted to eat some of that sweet green grass. So he decided to cross the bridge just like this.

Chorus: Trip trap. Trip trap. Trippity, trippity, trap.

Tangram: (Goat 1)

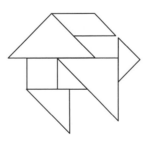

Storyteller 4: Suddenly, out from under the bridge appeared the willy wugly ugly troll! The troll roared,

Chorus: Who's that trippity trapping over my bridge?
Who's that trippity trapping over my bridge?

Storyteller 5: Little Billy Goat Gruff answered, "It is I, Little Billy Goat Gruff." The troll said, "Well, Little Billy Goat Gruff. You will make a mighty fine supper!" Little Billy Goat Gruff said, "I'm not fat enough. Wait for my brother." So the troll waited under the bridge.

Tangram: (Bridge)

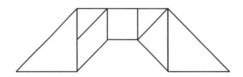

Storyteller 6: Middle Billy Goat Gruff saw sweet green grass on the other side. He wanted to eat some of that sweet green grass. So he decided to cross the bridge just like this.

Chorus: Trip trap. Trip trap. Trippity, trippity, trap.

Tangram: (Goat 2)

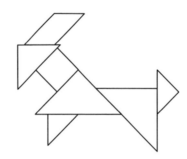

Storyteller 7: Suddenly, out from under the bridge appeared the willy wugly ugly troll! The troll roared,

Chorus: Who's that trippity trapping over my bridge?
Who's that trippity trapping over my bridge?

Storyteller 8: Middle Billy Goat Gruff answered, "It is I, Middle Billy Goat Gruff." The troll said, "Well, Middle Billy Goat Gruff. You will make a mighty fine supper!" Middle Billy Goat Gruff said, "I'm not fat enough. Wait for my brother." So the troll waited under the bridge.

Tangram: (Bridge)

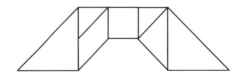

The Three Billy Goats Gruff (Page 3)

Storyteller 9:   Then Big Billy Goat Gruff saw sweet green grass on the other side. He wanted to eat some of that sweet green grass. So he decided to cross the bridge just like this.

Chorus: [Big voices] Trip trap. Trip trap. Trippity, trippity, trap.

Tangram: (Goat 3)

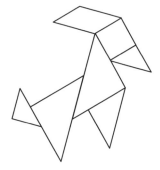

Storyteller 10:   Suddenly, out from under the bridge appeared the willy wugly ugly troll! The troll roared,

Chorus: Who's that trippity trapping over my bridge?
Who's that trippity trapping over my bridge?

Storyteller 11:   Big Billy Goat Gruff answered, "It is I, Big Billy Goat Gruff." The troll said, "Well, Big Billy Goat Gruff. You will make a mighty fine supper!" Big Billy Goat Gruff said, "Is that so?" He charged at the troll with his mighty horns and tossed that troll into the cold, deep river, next to a man in a boat.

Tangram: (Man in a boat)

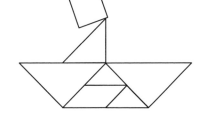

Storyteller 12:   Since then, no one has heard from that willy wugly ugly troll. And the three Billy Goats Gruff cross the bridge every day just like this.

Chorus: Trip trap. Trip trap. Trippity, trippity, trap.

Tangram: (Goat)

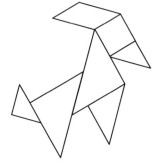

From *Tangram Tales: Story Theater Using the Ancient Chinese Puzzle* by Dianne de Las Casas. Westport, CT: Teacher Ideas Press. Copyright © 2009.

The Tiger and the Rabbit
Korea

Storyteller 1: A hungry tiger was walking through the wood when he saw a baby rabbit. The tiger was excited to find such a delicious meal. He said to the rabbit, "I'm going to eat you up."

Tangram: (Rabbit)

Chorus: Tasty, tasty, little bunny.
Yummy, yummy in my tummy!

Storyteller 2: The baby rabbit, although he was small, was quite clever. He said, "Mr. Tiger, I am still too young to make a good meal. I have something much tastier for you. I shall toast ten delicious rice cakes over a fire." The rabbit secretly picked up eleven small white stones and set them in a red-hot fire.

Tangram: (Fire)

Storyteller 3: As the stones became hot, the baby rabbit said, "Wait here and I'll get you some soy sauce to go with them. Do not eat any while I am gone. There are ten rice cakes toasting in the fire." Then the little rabbit hopped away into the wood. The tiger licked his lips. He was so hungry!

Tangram: (Rice cakes)

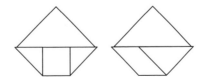

Storyteller 4: As soon as the rabbit was gone, Tiger counted eleven rice cakes toasting in the fire. "The baby rabbit said there were ten. He won't notice one missing."

Chorus: Tasty, tasty, sweet rice cakes.
Rabbit won't notice how much I ate!

Storyteller 4: So the greedy tiger took the reddest one from the fire and popped it in his mouth. It burned his tongue, it burned his throat, and then it burned his stomach. It was quite some time before Tiger could eat again.

Tangram: (Tiger)

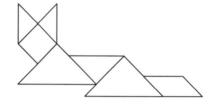

Storyteller 5: Some time later, Tiger happened upon the baby rabbit again. He said, "Baby rabbit, you tricked me once but not again. I am going to eat you up!"

Tangram: (Rabbit sitting)

Chorus: Tasty, tasty, little bunny.
Yummy, yummy in my tummy!

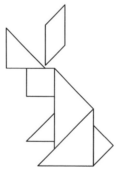

Storyteller 6: The baby rabbit was not a bit frightened. He said, "Mr. Tiger, I am still too young to make a good meal. I have something much tastier for you. I will show you how to catch thousands of sparrows. All you have to do is look at the sky and keep your mouth wide open."

Tangram: (Sparrow)

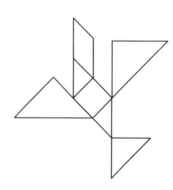

The Tiger and the Rabbit (Page 3)

Storyteller 7: So the greedy tiger opened his mouth wide and looked at the sky as the baby rabbit scampered away. Baby rabbit pretended to be shooing sparrows in Tiger's direction. Meanwhile, the rabbit set fire to a dry pile of leaves and twigs. Tiger thought,

Tangram: (Tiger sitting)

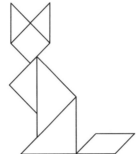

Chorus: Tasty, tasty birds for me!
How many sparrows will there be?

Storyteller 8: Tiger heard a roaring sound and then felt heat. Imagine his surprise to find fire, not sparrows, flying towards him! Tiger ran through the burning woods, singeing his striped coat. It was quite some time before he was covered in fur again.

Tangram: (Tiger running)

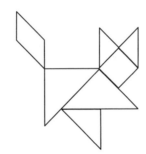

Storyteller 9: It was the beginning of winter when Tiger saw the baby rabbit again. He said, "Baby rabbit, you tricked me twice but not again. I am going to eat you up!"

Tangram: (Rabbit standing)

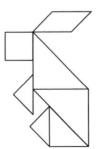

Chorus: Tasty, tasty, little bunny.
Yummy, yummy in my tummy!

The Tiger and the Rabbit (Page 4)

Storyteller 10: The baby rabbit was not a bit frightened. He said, "Mr. Tiger, I am still too young to make a good meal. I have something much tastier for you. I will show you how to catch huge fish with your tail. All you have to do is place your tail in the river, sit very still, and wait for the fish to bite."

Tangram: (Fish)

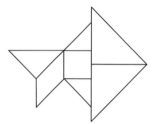

Chorus: Tasty, tasty little fish.
I'm going to eat this scrumptious dish!

Storyteller 11: The baby rabbit scampered away as the greedy tiger dipped his tail in the river. He sat and sat and sat, waiting for the fish to bite. Finally, he tried to get up but he couldn't move! He was stuck! His tail was frozen in the river. Tiger said, "That rabbit tricked me again!"

Tangram: (Tiger sitting upright)

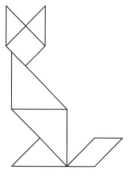

Storyteller 12: No matter how much Tiger tried to escape, it was useless. The next morning, the villagers found Tiger frozen solid. He was taken away, and the baby rabbit never again had to worry about being eaten by the greedy tiger.

From *Tangram Tales: Story Theater Using the Ancient Chinese Puzzle* by Dianne de Las Casas. Westport, CT: Teacher Ideas Press. Copyright © 2009.

The Tiger, the Brahman, and the Jackal
India

Storyteller 1: Once long ago, there was a tiger who had been caught in a trap. Try as he might, he could not escape.

Tangram: (Tiger clawing)

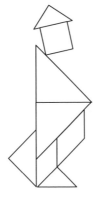

Storyteller 2: A short while later, a Brahman was walking by.

Tangram: (Man walking)

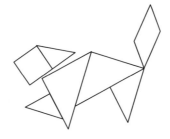

Storyteller 3: When the tiger saw the Brahman, he pleaded. "Please let me out! I would be eternally grateful!"

Storyteller 4: The Brahman said, "I cannot let you out. You will eat me." But the tiger promised the Brahman he would spare his life if the Brahman would release him. Foolishly, the Brahman agreed and released the tiger from the cage.

Chorus: ROAR!

Storyteller 5: The Brahman tried to run away, but the tiger caught him and said, "Now I will eat you!"

Tangram: (Man running) & (Tiger standing)

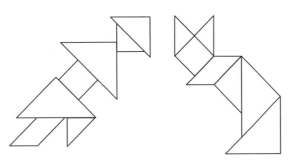

The Tiger, the Brahman, and the Jackal

Storyteller 6: The Brahman begged the tiger not to eat him. He said, "Let me ask the first three things I meet what they think. I will abide by their decision." The tiger agreed, and the Brahman set off on his journey.

Chorus: The Brahman walked (clap, clap) and he walked (clap, clap).
And he walked (clap, clap) and he walked (clap, clap).

Tangram: (Man walking)

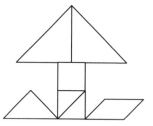

Storyteller 7: The first thing he saw was a large pipal tree. The Brahman asked the pipal tree for his opinion on the matter.

Tangram: (Pipal tree)

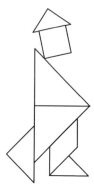

Storyteller 8: The pipal tree grumbled, "Why are you asking me? All day I give shade to passersby. They don't even thank me! All they do is tear off my limbs to feed to their cattle. Don't whimper. Be a man!" The poor Brahman was distraught, so he continued on.

Chorus: The Brahman walked (clap, clap) and he walked (clap, clap).
And he walked (clap, clap) and he walked (clap, clap).

Tangram: (Man walking)

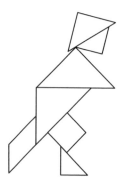

Storyteller 9:   The second thing the Brahman saw was a water buffalo. The Brahman asked the water buffalo for his opinion on the matter.

Tangram: (Water buffalo)

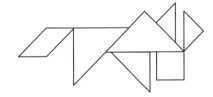

Storyteller 10:   The water buffalo grumbled, "Why are you asking me? When I gave milk, my owners fed me nothing but cotton-seed and oil-cake. Now that I am old and dry, they feed me nothing but scraps. Don't whimper. Be a man!" The poor Brahman was distraught, so he continued on.

Chorus: The Brahman walked (clap, clap) and he walked (clap, clap).
And he walked (clap, clap) and he walked (clap, clap).

Tangram: (Man walking)

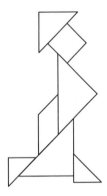

Storyteller 11:   The third thing the Brahman saw was the road. The Brahman asked the road for his opinion on the matter.

Tangram: (Road)

Storyteller 12:   The road grumbled, "Why are you asking me? I am useful to everyone, rich or poor. But I don't get gratitude! All I get are their discarded husks and ashes. Don't whimper. Be a man!" The poor Brahman was distraught, so he continued on.

Chorus: The Brahman walked (clap, clap) and he walked (clap, clap).
And he walked (clap, clap) and he walked (clap, clap).

The Tiger, the Brahman, and the Jackal

Storyteller 13: He was so upset that he didn't notice where he was going. The Brahman bumped into a jackal. The jackal asked, "What is wrong?" When the Brahman shared his story, the jackal said he would pass judgment if he could see where it all happened in the first place.

Tangram: (Jackal)

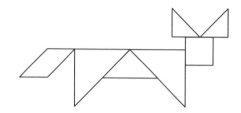

Chorus: So they walked (clap, clap) and they walked (clap, clap).
And they walked (clap, clap) and they walked (clap, clap).

Storyteller 14: When they came to the cage, the tiger was waiting. "I'm hungry!" the tiger roared. The jackal said, "Just a moment, sir. Would you please repeat the story to me so that I may decide this matter?" The tiger repeated the same story as the Brahman.

Storyteller 14: When the tiger was finished, the jackal said, "I'm confused. Would you mind showing me exactly how you were inside the cage?" The tiger walked into the cage, and as soon as he did
. . .

Chorus: SNAP!

Storyteller 14: The jackal shut the cage and locked it. The tiger was not happy.

Chorus: ROAR!

Tangram: (Closed cage)

Storyteller 15: But the Brahman and the jackal were!

Chorus: And they laughed (clap, clap) and they laughed (clap, clap).
And they laughed (clap, clap) and they laughed (clap, clap).

Storyteller 15: From that time on, the Brahman never let a tiger out of his cage. And neither should you!

Tiger's Tale, Anansi's Stories
West Indies

Chorus: Feel the story beat (clap, clap).
Feel the story beat (clap, clap).

Storyteller 1:   Before the world was as it is today, Tiger was the king of the forest. Because Tiger ruled the forest, many things were named after him. The lily with red stripes was called a tiger lily. The moth with striped wings was called a tiger moth. And the stories of the forest were called Tiger's Tales.

Tangram: (Tiger)

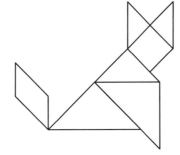

Storyteller 2:   Anansi the Spider was the weakest animal in the forest. He longed for greatness. One day he decided to approach Tiger to ask for a favor. Tiger kept his stories in a basket, and Anansi wanted the stories in the basket to be named after him.

Tangram: (Spider)

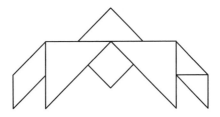

Storyteller 3:   Anansi bowed before Tiger and said, "Tiger, I have a favor to ask of you." Tiger asked, "What is it, Anansi?" Anansi answered, "Since you are king and have so many things named after you, I would like to have something named after me too. I would like the stories to be called 'Anansi Stories.'"

Chorus: Feel the story beat (clap, clap).
Feel the story beat (clap, clap)

Tangram: (Basket)

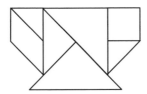

From *Tangram Tales: Story Theater Using the Ancient Chinese Puzzle* by Dianne de Las Casas. Westport, CT: Teacher Ideas Press. Copyright © 2009.

Storyteller 4: Lying in a leisurely position, Tiger said, "Very well, Anansi. But first you must complete two tasks. Bring me a gourd filled with bees. Then capture and bring me Snake. If you complete these tasks, I shall give you the story basket and name the stories 'Anansi Stories.'"

Chorus: Feel the story beat (clap, clap).
Feel the story beat (clap, clap).

Tangram: (Tiger lying down)

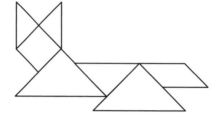

Storyteller 5: The next day, Anansi found an empty gourd and carried it to where the bees lived. Queen Bee asked, "Anansi, what are you doing with that gourd?" Anansi said, "I have made a foolish bet with Tiger. I am supposed to tell him how many bees this gourd can hold." Queen Bee said, "That is easy. I will help you. You will count as the bees fly in one by one. When the gourd is full, we will fly back out."

Tangram: (Bee)

Storyteller 6: Anansi said, "Excellent idea!" So the bees flew in one by one, and when the gourd was full, Anansi corked the opening. He brought the buzzing gourd to Tiger. Tiger was not happy. He did not think Anansi could complete the task. Anansi said, "I have one more task to complete and you will have to name the stories 'Anansi Stories.'"

Chorus: Feel the story beat (clap, clap).
Feel the story beat (clap, clap).

Tangram: (Gourd)

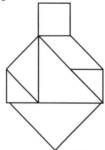

Storyteller 7: The next day, Anansi saw Snake and said, "Oh, no! What am I to do?" Snake asked, "What is wrong, Anansi?" Anansi answered, "I have made a foolish bet with Tiger. I am supposed to tell him if you are longer than this bamboo stick. But how will I measure you?" Snake said, "That is easy. I will help you. I will stretch out straight, next to the stick. You will see that I am longer than the stick."

Tangram: (Snake)

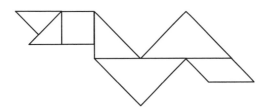

Storyteller 8: Snake stretched and stretched, but the stick was longer. As Snake stretched, Anansi quickly tied Snake to the bamboo. Snake was trapped! Anansi brought Snake to Tiger. Tiger was not happy, but he had to honor his word. Tiger gave the story basket to Anansi and named the stories after him. Since that time, Tiger's Tales have become known as Anansi's Stories.

Chorus: Feel the story beat (clap, clap).
Feel the story beat (clap, clap).

Tangram: (Spider)

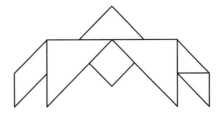

Storyteller 9: You may not be able to catch a tiger by the tale, but you can always catch Anansi spinning a splendid story. One more time!

Chorus: Feel the story beat (clap, clap).
Feel the story beat (clap, clap).

Too Much Nose
Italy

Storyteller 1: In the Italian countryside, there once lived a poor man who had three sons. He said, "Sons, it is time to seek your fortune. I have a gift for each of you." To the first son he gave a tattered coin purse.

Tangram: (Purse)

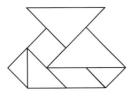

Storyteller 2: The first son said, "Father, it is old and no good." The father answered, "It is a magic coin purse. Each time you reach in, you will always receive a coin." To the second son he gave a ragged hat.

Tangram: (Hat)

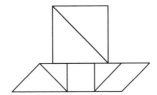

Storyteller 3: The second son said, "Father, it is old and no good." The father answered, "It is a magic hat. It makes the wearer invisible." To the third son he gave a rusty horn.

Tangram: (Horn)

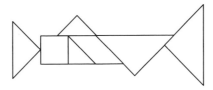

Storyteller 4: The third son said, "Father, it is old and no good." The father answered, "It is a magic horn. When you blow it, it will give you whatever you need, whether it is food, clothes, or an army. Now go and do not tell anyone about your magic objects." So the three sons left. The first son passed in front of a palace.

Too Much Nose (Page 2)

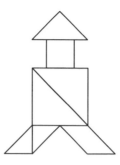

Tangram: (Palace)

Storyteller 5:   A servant from the palace said to the first son, "The queen needs a card player." So the first son went inside the palace to play cards with the queen.

Tangram: (Queen on throne)

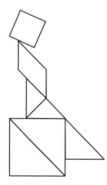

Storyteller 6:   The queen won the card game and ordered the boy to pay 30 pieces of silver. The boy reached into his coin purse 30 times and pulled out 30 pieces of silver. When the queen asked how he did that, the boy said, "It is a magic coin purse with a never-ending supply of coins."

Chorus: The queen cried, "It's mine. It's mine. It's mine I say!"
                 She grabbed the magic coin purse and took it away.

Tangram: (Coin purse)

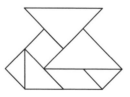

Storyteller 7:   The next day, the first son visited his brother. He borrowed the magic hat and became invisible. He went back to the palace and drank all of the queen's soup before her eyes. The queen cried out, "What is going on?" The invisible boy said, "Return my coin purse." The queen answered, "I will when I can see you." So the boy took off the magic hat. When the queen asked how he became invisible, the boy said, "It is a magic hat that makes the wearer invisible."

Chorus: The queen cried, "It's mine. It's mine. It's mine I say!"
She grabbed the magic hat and took it away.

Tangram: (Hat)

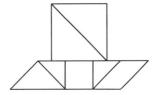

Storyteller 8: The next day, the first son visited his other brother and borrowed the magic horn. He went back to the palace and blew the horn, calling for an army. The queen cried out, "What is going on?" The boy said, "Return my coin purse and my hat." The queen answered, "I will if you come inside." So the boy went inside the palace. When the queen asked how he called the army with his horn, the boy said, "It is a magic horn that gives you whatever you need, whether it is food, clothes, or an army."

Chorus: The queen cried, "It's mine. It's mine. It's mine I say!"
She grabbed the magic horn and took it away.

Tangram: (Horn)

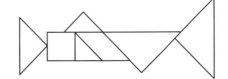

Storyteller 9: The first son was very upset, so he wandered until he came to a grove of fig trees. Feeling hungry, he grabbed a fig and ate it. To his dismay, his nose began to grow.

Chorus: His nose grew and grew and grew.
The boy didn't know what to do!

Tangram: (Boy with big nose)

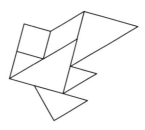

Storyteller 9: He ran until he came to a grove of cherry trees. Feeling hungry, he grabbed a cherry and ate it. To his delight, his nose began to shrink. "Now I know what to do!" He picked a basket full of figs and bottled the cherry juice. The first son walked back to the palace.

Too Much Nose (Page 4)

Tangram: (Boy walking)

Storyteller 10:   When he reached the palace, he cried, "Figs for sale! Figs for sale!" The queen's servants bought the whole basket and brought it inside. The queen and her servants began eating the figs. To their dismay, their noses began to grow!

Chorus: Their noses grew and grew and grew.
                 The servants didn't know what to do!

Tangram: (Man with big nose)

Storyteller 11:   The first son disguised himself as a doctor and yelled, "Nose medicine for sale! Nose medicine for sale!" The queen ordered that the doctor be summoned to the palace. Once inside, the boy dropped the cherry juice on all the servants' noses and they returned to normal size. The queen said, "That medicine may be magic, but I have even greater magic! I have a magic coin purse with a never-ending supply of coins, a magic hat that makes its wearer invisible, and a magic horn that can call an army!" The boy said, "Show me." As soon as the queen did . . .

Chorus: The boy cried, "It's mine. It's mine. It's mine I say!"
                 He grabbed the magic objects and took them away.

Storyteller 12:   The boy ran as fast as he could with his magic objects and his magic cherry juice, leaving the queen with . . .

Chorus: TOO MUCH NOSE!

Storyteller 12:   From that time on, the three brothers took good care of their magic objects and stayed far away from the palace. The end.

Tangram: (Palace)

The Traveling Fox
England

Storyteller 1: A fox was digging behind a stump when he found a bumblebee. The fox put the bumblebee into a sack and began traveling.

Tangram: (Bee)

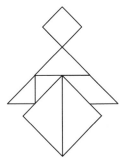

Storyteller 2: When the fox came upon a house, he knocked on the door. He said to the mistress of the house, "May I leave my sack here while I go to Squintum's?" The woman said, "Yes." The fox warned, "Be careful not to open the sack."

Tangram: (House)

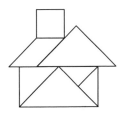

Storyteller 3: As soon as the fox was out of sight, the woman peeked inside the sack and the bee flew out. The rooster jumped up and ate the bee. After a while, the fox came back. He asked, "Where is my bumblebee?" The woman answered, "I untied the sack, the bee flew out, and the rooster ate him." The fox said, "Very well. I must have the rooster." So he caught the rooster and said,

Chorus: Get into my sack
Just like that!
Then the fox began traveling.

Tangram: (Rooster)

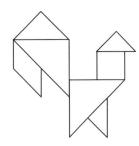

Storyteller 4: When the fox came upon the next house, he knocked on the door. He said to the mistress of the house, "May I leave my bag here while I go to Squintum's?" The woman said, "Yes." The fox warned, "Be careful not to open the sack."

Tangram: (House)

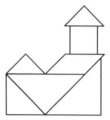

Storyteller 5: As soon as the fox was out of sight, the woman peeked inside the sack and the rooster flew out. The pig jumped up and ate the rooster. After a while, the fox came back. He asked, "Where is my rooster?" The woman answered, "I untied the sack, the rooster flew out, and the pig ate him." The fox said, "Very well. I must have the pig." So he caught the pig and said,

Chorus: Get into my sack
Just like that!
Then the fox began traveling.

Tangram: (Pig)

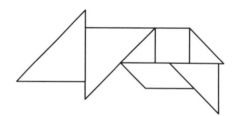

Storyteller 6: When the fox came upon the next house, he knocked on the door. He said to the mistress of the house, "May I leave my bag here while I go to Squintum's?" The woman said, "Yes." The fox warned, "Be careful not to open the sack."

Tangram: (House)

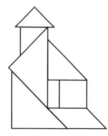

Storyteller 7: As soon as the fox was out of sight, the woman peeked inside the sack and the pig flew out. The ox jumped up and ate the pig. After a while, the fox came back. He asked, "Where is my pig?" The woman answered, "I untied the sack, the pig flew out, and the ox ate him." The fox said, "Very well. I must have the ox." So he caught the ox and said,

Chorus: Get into my sack
Just like that!
Then the fox began traveling.

Tangram: (Ox)

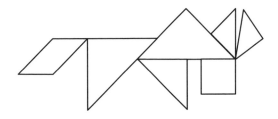

Storyteller 8: When the fox came upon the next house, he knocked on the door. He said to the mistress of the house, "May I leave my bag here while I go to Squintum's?" The woman said, "Yes." The fox warned, "Be careful not to open the sack."

Tangram: (House)

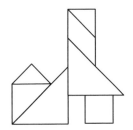

Storyteller 9: As soon as the fox was out of sight, the woman peeked inside the sack and the ox flew out. Her boy jumped up and chased the ox. After a while, the fox came back. He asked, "Where is my ox?" The woman answered, "I untied the sack, the ox flew out, and my boy chased him into the field." The fox said, "Very well. I must have the boy." So he caught the boy and said,

Chorus: Get into my sack
Just like that!
Then the fox began traveling.

Tangram: (Boy)

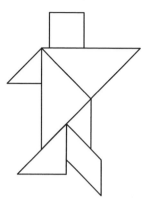

Storyteller 8:   When the fox came upon the next house, he knocked on the door. He said to the mistress of the house, "May I leave my bag here while I go to Squintum's?" The woman said, "Yes." The fox warned, "Be careful not to open the sack."

Tangram: (House)

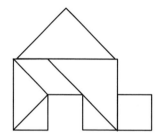

Storyteller 9:   The woman was baking a cake and her children were begging for a piece. The boy inside the sack smelled the cake and began to cry for a piece. The woman untied the sack, let the boy out, and placed the house-dog in the sack. When the fox returned, he saw that his bag was tied fast, so he put it over his back and began traveling. Once in the woods, he opened the sack. Imagine his surprise when the dog flew out!

Chorus: The little boy was safe and sound.
While the fox made dinner for the hound.

Tangram: (Fox)

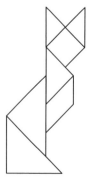

Windbird and the Sun
South Africa

Storyteller 1:   A story, a story. Let it come! Let it go! Thashira, the daughter of a queen, was a beautiful girl, but nothing made her happy except bright colors. Thashira thought that color brought beauty to the world. But she lived in the dry country and her surroundings were dull and bare, so Thashira never smiled.

Chorus: Red, orange, yellow, green, blue, violet swirl.
Colors, bright colors make a beautiful world!

Tangram: (Sad woman)

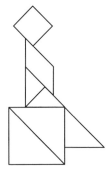

Storyteller 2:   One day Thashira looked up and saw the sky. It was a soft azure color. Thashira's heart danced with joy and she smiled! When she smiled, Sun noticed. His colorful sky made Thashira happy, and Thashira's warm smile made Sun happy. Soon, they became very fond of each other.

Chorus: Red, orange, yellow, green, blue, violet swirl.
Colors, bright colors make a beautiful world!

Tangram: (Sun)

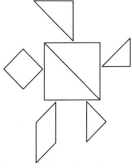

Storyteller 3:   Every day, Thashira climbed to the highest koppie to see the new colors Sun would place in the sky. Every day, Sun gazed upon Thashira and her warm smile. It wasn't long before he fell in love with her.

Chorus: Red, orange, yellow, green, blue, violet swirl.
Colors, bright colors make a beautiful world!

Tangram: (Small mountain)

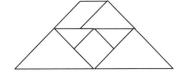

From *Tangram Tales: Story Theater Using the Ancient Chinese Puzzle* by Dianne de Las Casas. Westport, CT: Teacher Ideas Press. Copyright © 2009.

Storyteller 4: One day Thashira was gazing into the sky when Windbird saw her pretty face and warm smile. Windbird fell in love with Thashira. He blew a soft gentle wind across her face and through her hair, but Thashira never noticed.

Tangram: (Flying bird with big wings)

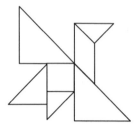

Storyteller 5: Windbird blew gently for weeks. He tore off pieces of gray clouds and brought them from far away. The heavy clouds sprinkled soft rains upon the dry country. Soon, flowers blossomed and plants flourished. There were colors of every kind for Thashira to enjoy.

Chorus: Red, orange, yellow, green, blue, violet swirl.
Colors, bright colors make a beautiful world!

Tangram: (Flower blooming)

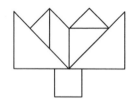

Storyteller 6: But Thashira was so busy gazing at Sun and the sky that she never noticed Windbird's efforts. Windbird decided to impress Thashira with his strength. He cried, "Thashira, it is I who made the grass and flowers grow so that you could enjoy their colors. Now behold my strength!" Windbird whistled wildly and blew big gusts across the veld. His strong winds flattened the grass, tore the flowers, and uprooted the bushes.

Tangram: (Bird with wings outstretched)

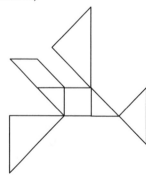

Storyteller 7: When Windbird was finished, Thashira looked around. The destruction of the land and the disappearance of the colors saddened her. When Windbird called on her, she shooed him away. She lay quietly under the baobab tree.

Tangram: (Tree)

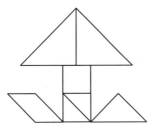

Storyteller 8: The queen noticed how sad her daughter was. She asked, "Thashira, what will make you happy again?" Thashira answered, "To be with Sun, for he fills the sky with bright colors and helps the beautiful flowers bloom."

Chorus: Red, orange, yellow, green, blue, violet swirl.
Colors, bright colors make a beautiful world!

Tangram: (Sun)

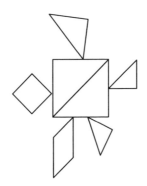

Storyteller 9: The queen said, "Very well. It shall be done." She ordered that a great ladder be built, tall enough to reach the sky. The people began building. Even the animals helped—elephants, hippos, rhinos, and monkeys. Everyone worked hard to build the great ladder.

Tangram: (Ladder)

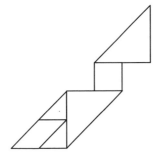

Windbird and the Sun (Page 4)

Storyteller 10:   When the ladder was finished, Thashira began climbing toward the sky. When Windbird found out, he was furious. He thrashed and thundered, "We shall see who is strongest—Wind or Sun!" The queen cried as the ladder crumbled to the ground. But Thashira did not fall. She floated to the sky into the arms of her beloved Sun.

Tangram: (Woman flying or reaching)

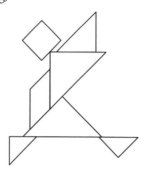

Storyteller 11:   The queen looked up and saw Sun in all his brilliance. Next to him was Thashira, shimmering in bold, beautiful colors. Thashira became a rainbow. No matter how hard Windbird blows, Rainbow shines bright, bringing beauty to the world with her colors. A story, a story. Let it come. Let it go.

Chorus: Red, orange, yellow, green, blue, violet swirl.
Colors, bright colors make a beautiful world!

Tangram: (Rainbow)

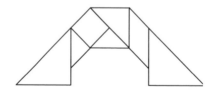

Source Notes

"The Bossy Rooster" was adapted from *The Bossy Gallito* by Lucia M. Gonzalez (New York: Scholastic Press, 1994) and "The Elegant Rooster" in *Multicultural Folktales: Stories to Tell Young Children* by Judy Sierra and Robert Kaminski (Phoenix, AZ: Oryx Press, 1991).

"The Cat and the Rooster" was adapted from "The Cat and the Rooster" in *Around the World in 80 Tales* by Nicola Baxter (Norwich, United Kingdom: Bookmark Limited, 2002).

"The Fox's Daughter" was adapted from "The Fox's Daughter" in *The Arbuthnot Anthology of Children's Literature, Third Edition,* edited by May Hill Arbuthnot (Glenview, Illinois: Scott, Foresman and Company, 1961).

"The Goat in the Jalapeño Patch" was adapted from "The Goat in the Chile Patch" in *Multicultural Folktales: Stories to Tell Young Children* by Judy Sierra and Robert Kaminski (Phoenix, AZ: Oryx Press, 1991).

"Grandfather Rabbit and the Foolish Fox" was adapted from "Chief-Grandfather Rabbit and the Foolish Fox" in *Tales from Around the World* by Graham Percy (New York: Barnes & Noble Books, 2003).

"Grandmother Spider" was adapted from "Grandmother Spider" in *The Dial Book of Animal Tales from Around the World* by Naomi Adler (New York: Dial Books for Young Readers, 1996).

"The Greedy Frog" was adapted from "The Greedy Frog" in *The Dial Book of Animal Tales from Around the World* by Naomi Adler (New York: Dial Books for Young Readers, 1996).

"Henny Penny" was adapted from "Henny Penny" in *English Fairy Tales* by Joseph Jacobs (New York: Alfred A. Knopf, 1993; first published in 1890) and "Henny-Penny" in *The Arbuthnot Anthology of Children's Literature, Third Edition,* edited by May Hill Arbuthnot (Glenview, Illinois: Scott, Foresman and Company, 1961).

"The Hodja's Bet" was adapted from *Tales of the Hodja: The Bet* by C. W. Gilchrist (Istanbul, Turkey: Metro Book Publishing, 1989) and "The Bet" in *202 Jokes of Nasreddin Hodja* (Istanbul, Turkey: Minyatur Yayinlari, n.d.).

"The House That Jack Built" was adapted from "This Is the House That Jack Built" in *Mother Goose,* edited by Eulalie Osgood Grover (Franklin, Tennessee: Dalmatian Press, 2000).

"It Could Always Be Worse!" was adapted from *It Could Always Be Worse* by Margot Zemach (New York: Farrar, Straus and Giroux, 1976) and *Too Much Noise* by Ann McGovern (New York: Houghton Mifflin Company, 1992).

"Jack Seeks His Fortune" was adapted from "How Jack Went to Seek His Fortune" in *Troll Treasury of Animal Stories,* edited by John C. Miles (Mahwah, New Jersey: Troll Associates, 1991); "The Musicians of Bremen" in *The Dial Book of Animal Tales from Around the World* by Naomi Adler (New York: Dial Books for Young Readers, 1996); and "How Jack Went to Seek His Fortune" in *English Fairy Tales* by Joseph Jacobs (New York: Alfred A. Knopf, 1993; first published in 1890).

"La Cucarachita Martina" was adapted from "La Cucarachita Martina" in *An Illustrated Treasury of Latino Read-Aloud Stories* by Maite Suarez-Riva (New York: Black Dog & Leventhal Publishers, 2004).

"The Mitten" was adapted from *The Mitten* by Alvin Tresselt (New York: Lothrop, Lee & Shepard Co., 1964) and *The Mitten* by Jan Brett (New York: G. P. Putnam's Sons, 1989).

"The Old Woman and Her Pig" was adapted from "The Old Woman and Her Pig" in *English Fairy Tales* by Joseph Jacobs (New York: Alfred A. Knopf, 1993; first published in 1890); *The Arbuthnot Anthology of Children's Literature, Third Edition,* edited by May Hill Arbuthnot (Glenview, Illinois: Scott, Foresman and Company, 1961); and "The Old Woman and Her Pig" in *Troll Treasury of Animal Stories,* edited by John C. Miles (Mahwah, New Jersey: Troll Associates, 1991).

"Rabbit's Turnip" was adapted from *Rabbit's Gift* by George Shannon (New York: Harcourt 2007).

"Silly Ivan's Salt" was adapted from "Salt" in *Timeless Tales from Many Lands,* edited by Susan Randol (New York: The Reader's Digest Association, 2001).

"The Stonecutter" was adapted from "The Stonecutter" in *Multicultural Folktales: Stories to Tell Young Children* by Judy Sierra and Robert Kaminski (Phoenix, AZ: Oryx Press, 1991); "The Stonecutter" by Andrew Lang in *The Crimson Fairy Book* (London: Longmans, Green, and Company, 1903); and "The Stonecutter" from Professor D. L. Ashliman's Folktexts, http://www.pitt.edu/~dash/japan.html#stonecutter.

"The Three Billy Goats Gruff" was adapted from "The Three Billy-Goats Gruff" in *The Arbuthnot Anthology of Children's Literature, Third Edition,* edited by May Hill Arbuthnot (Glenview, Illinois: Scott, Foresman and Company, 1961) and "Three Billy Goats Gruff" in *Troll Treasury of Animal Stories,* edited by John C. Miles (Mahwah, New Jersey: Troll Associates, 1991).

"The Tiger and the Rabbit" was adapted from "The Tiger and the Rabbit" in *Korean Children's Favorite Stories* by Kim So-un (Boston: Tuttle Publishing, 1955).

"The Tiger, the Brahman, and the Jackal" was adapted from "The Tiger, the Old Man and the Jackal" in *Tales from Around the World* by Graham Percy (New York: Barnes & Noble Books, 2003); "The Tiger, Brahman, and the Jackal" in *The Arbuthnot Anthology of Children's Literature, Third Edition,* edited by May Hill Arbuthnot (Glenview, Illinois: Scott, Foresman and Company, 1961); and "The Tiger, the Brahman and the Jackal" from *Indian Fairy Tales,* http://www.sacred-texts.com/hin/ift/ift10.htm.

"Tiger's Tale, Anansi's Stories" was adapted from *Spider and the Sky God* by Deborah M. Newton Chocolate (Mahwah, New Jersey: Troll Associates, 1993); "How Spider Obtained the Sky-God's Stories" in *Best-Loved Folktales of the World,* selected by Joanna Cole (New York: Doubleday, 1982); and "Why the Stories Belong to Ananse" by Dale Pepin on the Story Socks Web site, http://user1291600.sites.myregisteredsite.com/library/id80.html.

"Too Much Nose" was adapted from *Too Much Nose: An Italian Tale* by Harve Zemach (New York: Reader's Digest Services, 1967); "The Long-Nosed Princess" in *Korean Folk-tales* retold by James Riordan (Oxford: Oxford University Press, 1994); and *The Greedy Princess,* adapted by Duance Vorhees & Mark Mueller (Elizabeth, New Jersey: Hollym International Corp., 1990).

"The Traveling Fox" was adapted from "The Travels of a Fox" in *Multicultural Folktales: Stories to Tell Young Children* by Judy Sierra and Robert Kaminski (Phoenix, AZ: Oryx Press, 1991); "The Travels of a Fox" in *The Arbuthnot Anthology of Children's Literature, Third Edition,* edited by May Hill Arbuthnot (Glenview, Illinois: Scott, Foresman and Company, 1961); and "The Travels of a Fox" from *The Baldwin Project: For the Children's Story Hour* by Carolyn S. Bailey, http://www.mainlesson.com/display.php?author = bailey&book = hour&story = travels.

"Windbird and the Sun" was adapted from "Windbird and the Sun" in *The Arbuthnot Anthology of Children's Literature, Third Edition,* edited by May Hill Arbuthnot (Glenview, Illinois: Scott, Foresman and Company, 1961).

Resources

Tangram Books

Grandfather Tang's Story by Anne Tompert (New York: Dragonfly Books, 1997).

Story Puzzles: Tales in the Tangram Tradition by Valerie Marsh (Fort Atkinson, Wisconsin: Highsmith Press, 1996).

Tangram: 1,600 Ancient Chinese Puzzles by Joost Elffers and Michael Schuyt (New York: Barnes & Noble Books, 1997).

Tangrams by James Lyon (New York: Barnes & Noble Publishing, 2005).

Tangram Puzzles: 500 Tricky Shapes to Confound & Astound by Chris Crawford (New York: Sterling Publishing Co., 2002).

Three Pigs, One Wolf and Seven Magic Shapes by Grace Maccarone (New York: Cartwheel Books, 1998).

The Warlord's Puzzle by Virginia Walton Pilegard (Gretna, LA: Pelican Publishing Company, 2000).

Tangram Websites

Note: A Google search on Tangrams will yield numerous results, but these Websites are a few of my favorites.

Tangrams, http://tangrams.ca/.
>   This site has a lot of great Tangram puzzles and solutions and includes downloadable printouts.

Sagwa's Tangrams on PBS Kids, http://pbskids.org/sagwa/games/tangrams/index.html.
>   Sagwa, a PBS Kids cartoon, has a Website that includes a terrific interactive Tangram game.

Links Learning Tangram Lesson, http://www.linkslearning.org/Kids/1_Math/2_Illustrated_Lessons/7_Tangrams/.

This site has a fantastic instructional video on the Tangram, including instructions on how to cut a Tangram and a glossary of terms. Great for the classroom.

Where to Purchase Tangram Sets

Large, Magnetic Foam Tangrams

I purchased my set from Educational Insights, http://www.educationalinsights.com. The package comes with six Tangram sets in various colors—red, yellow, orange, green, blue, and purple.

32 Sets of Foam Tangrams (224 pieces)

This collection of 32 sets of tangrams comes in a large bucket and is perfect for the classroom. Purchase from Delta Education, http://www.delta-education.com.

About the Author

Photo credit: Randy Richards

Author and award-winning storyteller Dianne de Las Casas sizzles on stage with "traditional folklore gone fun!" and "revved-up storytelling." Audiences don't just listen—they sing, clap, dance, chant, and roar with laughter. De Las Casas adapts traditional folklore, adding audience participation, song, and, of course, humor. A dramatic storyteller, she does not stand still. Using character voices, creative movement, and animated facial expressions and gestures, she creates a world of fantasy and enchantment. Childhood travels around the world shaped her future as a storyteller. De Las Casas has lived in the Philippines, Hawaii, and Spain and has traveled across Europe and the United States. Her cultural experiences have nourished her imagination, and she continues to draw on that knowledge, adding depth and richness to her tales.

De Las Casas is a Louisiana State Roster Artist, a Louisiana Touring Directory Artist, and a Mississippi Arts Education Demonstration Roster Artist. She is the author of *Story Fest: Crafting Story Theater Scripts* (Teacher Ideas Press, 2005), *Kamishibai Story Theater: The Art of Picture Telling* (Teacher Ideas Press, 2006), *Handmade Tales: Stories to Make and Take* (Libraries Unlimited, 2008), *Tangram Tales: Story Theater Using the Ancient Chinese Puzzle* (Teacher Ideas Press, 2008), *The Story Biz Handbook: How to Manage Your Storytelling Career from the Desk to the Stage* (Libraries Unlimited, 2008), *The Cajun Cornbread Boy* (Pelican Publishing Co., 2009), and *Scared Silly: 25 Tales to Tickle and Thrill* (Libraries Unlimited, 2009).

Her debut CD, *Jambalaya—Stories with Louisiana Flavor,* won a 2004 iParenting Media Award, a 2004 Children's Music Web Award, and a 2005 Storytelling World Honor. In addition, *Jambalaya* received rave reviews in *School Library Journal, AudioFile Magazine, Kidzmusic.com,* and *Georgia Family Magazine.* Her second CD, *World Fiesta,* won a 2005 Children's Music Web Award and received a rave review in *ALA Booklist* and was selected by School Library Journal as "Audio of the Week." *Booklist* says, "De Las Casas' commanding voice, unique characterizations, emotive vocalizations, and creative methods of reaching out to her audience are most engaging." Her latest CD, *Jump, Jiggle & Jam—A Rhythmic Romp through Story Land,* won 2006 NAPPA Honors, a 2006 Children's Music Web Award, and rave reviews in *School Library Journal* and *Publisher's Weekly.*

She performs arts-in-education programs and residencies at schools, libraries, festivals, museums, and special events. A frequent presenter at IRA, ALA, AASL, and other literacy and education conferences, de Las Casas is also a sought-after international professional development workshop leader. She is an enthusiastic advocate of literacy and arts-in-education programming, and she continues to make the story connection with thousands of children every year, reaching and teaching through the wonder of stories.